DAWN OF REALITIES

Fight today for a better tomorrow

By

M.K JOUVENALLISS

Table of contents

Avowal

First of all, my greatest gratitude goes to the Almighty God. His Grace has been sufficient. To my dad and mum, Benedict and Victoria for their Heroic Parenting. My brothers and Sisters for always being there for me. The many leaders who inspired me in many different ways. My lovely Boys Brummelhuis and Beelbright for the concerted effort they accorded to me during the long hours of drafting and writing this book. And finally, to my lovely wife Zemenay who has been a central pillar in my life. A confidant who always inspired me to write, write and write. Thank you all may God bless you.

Dedication

I would like to dedicate this book to all fellow citizens who through their constitutional right and good will usually wake up early morning on an election day to vote for our leaders.

Those citizens who refuse the small bribes offered by greedy politicians to manipulate them so as to remain in power.

Those citizens who know and understand the power of unity, the pursuit of justice, and the triumph of hope in the face of overwhelming adversity.

Those citizens who are willing to unlock the shattered visions through the refusal of greedy leaders by accepting and embracing new eras of hope and restoration.

There is only one message for you. A message delivered with concern and pure love. The time is now. **"Fight today for a better tomorrow"**

Foreword

When I was approached to write the foreword for this remarkable book, I hesitated for a moment. As a seasoned journalist, I have witnessed the struggles and triumphs of African nations, the complexities of politics, and the devastating consequences of corruption. It is a topic that hits close to home, and I have seen its impact firsthand.

The story you are about to embark on is a powerful testament to the resilience of the human spirit and the fight for justice in the face of overwhelming odds. It delves deep into the dark underbelly of politics, shedding light on the all-too-common reality of politicians who prioritize personal gain over the welfare of the people they are meant to serve.

In this epic fiction, Jouvenalliss Mwendwa Kioko reflects on how to reshape the narrative of African communities and leaving a lasting legacy of transformation. With his vision and unwavering dedication, he is poised to redefine the very essence of leadership and the possibilities that could be achieved. He brings the characters of this gripping tale alive with a rawness that captures the essence of the African experience. The stark contrast between the opulent lifestyle of Mr. Masur's family and the struggles faced by Mr. Mutinda's family exposes the gaping divide within society. It is a divide that is all too familiar to many Africans, where the rich prosper at the expense of the impoverished.

Through the eyes of Lynne Carrow and Benjamin, we witness the transformative power of conscience and the courage to stand against corruption. Their love story, intertwined with their shared desire to bring change, becomes a beacon of hope amidst the darkness. It serves as a reminder that love can transcend boundaries and unite individuals in the pursuit of a common goal.

The pages of this book bear witness to the power of truth, the importance of unity, and the resilience of the human spirit. It is a rallying cry to all those who believe in a better future, a future where African politicians prioritize the needs of the people over personal gain.

As you embark on this journey, I implore you to keep an open heart and an open mind. Let the characters guide you through the labyrinth of corruption and deceit, and may their struggles inspire you to question the status quo, to demand accountability, and to envision a brighter tomorrow.

Together, let us shine a light on the dark corners, expose the web of corruption, and pave the way for a new era of African politics—one rooted in integrity, empathy, and the unwavering commitment to serve the people.

Foreword by Tekla MAXWELL,

Renowned Journalist and Advocate for Transparency.

Introduction

The sun dipped below the horizon, casting long shadows over the sprawling city, its golden rays fading into the twilight. Within the depths of this metropolis, where the contrast between opulence and destitution was stark, two families existed at opposite ends of the social spectrum.

In the affluent neighborhood, nestled behind high walls and ornate gates, resided the Masur family. Mr. Masur, a prominent member of parliament, wielded influence and power, his every move orchestrated to secure his position and safeguard his wealth. His wife, Clair, epitomized the materialistic desires that came with their elevated status, her days consumed by the pursuit of luxury and pleasure. Their son, Roy, grew up shielded from the harsh realities of the world, cocooned within a bubble of privilege and comfort. However, it was their eldest daughter, Lynne Carrow, who had begun to question the morality of her father's actions, the glaring disconnect between their lavish lifestyle and the suffering of their constituents.

Contrasting the Masur family's affluent existence was the Mutinda family, living in the squalor of the city's slums. Mr. Mutinda, burdened by the weight of his own demons, sought solace in the embrace of alcohol, drowning his dreams and aspirations in a haze of numbing intoxication. Esther, his wife, fought an uphill battle, resorting to selling illicit brew to keep their family afloat amidst the tides of poverty. Their son, Benjamin, carried within him a flame of determination, fueled by his deep empathy for the people around him. He loathed the corrupt practices of Mr. Masur, a man who had turned a blind eye to the struggles of his constituents. Benjamin's dreams of becoming a politician were driven by a sincere desire to uplift his people, to be the voice they so desperately needed.

These two families, seemingly worlds apart, were destined to collide. In a twist of fate, Lynne Carrow and Benjamin found themselves face-to-face at a debate symposium, their opposing ideals and shared convictions kindling a connection that defied their circumstances. Lynne Carrow's affections grew, the fire of her spirit yearning to break free from her father's shadow, to prove that she was different, that she genuinely desired change. But Benjamin, scarred by the injustices he had witnessed, struggled to trust her intentions, wary of her familial ties to the corrupt world he sought to dismantle.

Their lives would intertwine in ways neither could have foreseen. Lynne Carrow's quest for knowledge and understanding led her abroad, while Benjamin, fueled by his burning determination, started a small business within the slums, nurturing it into a thriving enterprise against all odds. Separated by distance, their shared passion for justice kept their hearts entwined, as they navigated the treacherous landscape of politics and power.

As Lynne Carrow returned to her homeland, armed with the knowledge she had acquired, her reunion with Benjamin marked the beginning of a formidable partnership. Together, they embarked on a campaign that aimed to shatter the status quo, to expose the corrupt underbelly of politics and ignite a flame of hope within their community. Their journey would be fraught with challenges, both personal and political, but they were armed with unwavering determination and the unyielding support of those who had grown tired of broken promises.

In the face of a system rigged against them, Lynne Carrow and Benjamin would wage a battle that would test the limits of their resilience. The struggle for justice, redemption, and love would push them to their limits, revealing the strength within their hearts and the power of unity in the face of adversity.

And so, the stage was set, and the curtain lifted on a story that would weave together the lives of these two families and the fate of an entire constituency. Their journey would be a testament to the indomitable human spirit, exploring themes of corruption, sacrifice, and the enduring power of hope.

As Lynne Carrow and Benjamin took their first steps into the world of politics, they began to unearth the true extent of the rot that had infected their community. Behind closed doors, they discovered the depths of Mr. Masur's corrupt practices, witnessing the web of bribes, embezzlement, and deceit that had kept him in power for far too long. Each revelation served as fuel for their righteous anger, driving them forward with an unwavering resolve to expose the truth.

But as their campaign gained momentum, their enemies grew more desperate. The Masur family, along with their network of cronies and beneficiaries, fought tooth and nail to protect their ill-gotten gains. Threats, intimidation, and even attempts to tarnish their reputations became commonplace. Yet, Lynne Carrow and Benjamin stood tall, their hearts fortified by the support of the oppressed citizens who had long yearned for change.

The battle for the hearts and minds of the people was fought on multiple fronts. Lynne Carrow, armed with her intelligence and persuasive eloquence, captivated audiences with her speeches, dissecting the flaws in the current system and painting a vivid picture of the future she envisioned. Benjamin, in contrast, took to the streets, immersing himself in the lives of the people he aimed to represent. He listened to their stories, their struggles, and their dreams, channeling their hopes into a powerful force that would shape their shared destiny.

The climax of their campaign approached with the looming election day. The air crackled with anticipation as the people prepared to cast their votes, their minds torn between the familiar promises of the past and the glimmer of hope embodied by Lynne Carrow and Benjamin. The day would not pass without its share of underhanded tactics and desperate attempts to sway the outcome, but the resilience of the people could not be underestimated.

When the final tally was counted, a wave of triumph surged through the hearts of the citizens. Benjamin emerged as the victor, dethroning the corrupt reign of Mr. Masur and paving the way for a new era of accountability and justice. The celebration that swept through the constituency was a testament to the power of unity and the belief that change was indeed possible.

Lynne Carrow and Benjamin's victory marked the beginning of a lifelong journey. As they stepped into their roles as representatives of the people, they faced the daunting task of rebuilding their community, healing the wounds inflicted by years of neglect. Guided by their unwavering dedication, they implemented policies and initiatives that prioritized the welfare of the citizens, ensuring that their voices were finally heard and their needs met.

In the midst of their shared mission, Lynne Carrow and Benjamin's bond grew stronger, their love becoming an anchor amidst the storms of politics. Together, they forged a partnership built on trust, mutual respect, and an unwavering commitment to serve their people.

"Dawn of realities" is a gripping tale of resilience and redemption, reminding us that the fight against corruption and injustice is a collective endeavor. It invites readers to question the status quo and envision a world where the pursuit of power is synonymous with the pursuit of justice and equality. Through the intertwined lives of Lynne Carrow, Benjamin, and the Masur and Mutinda families, this epic fiction novel serves as both a mirror reflecting the flaws in our society and a beacon of hope, illuminating the path towards a brighter future. So prepare to embark on a journey of intrigue, passion, and triumph as "Dawn of realities" transports you.

Chapter 1:

The Divide

Spot lights surrounded the tall walls of Nerak Estate. The climate was cool and the night itself could tell the opulence of the vicinity. Clair had just refreshened herself and sat at their huge stylish living room perhaps to watch the news. Lynne carrow who was standing at the front view balcony faltered to the sitting room, and sat direct opposite her mother. News started and the headline was: Members of parliament push for salary increment in the next financial year. Immediately Clair clapped her hands happily saying, "Your father is going to have a bigger wallet!"

"This is unacceptable even in the eyes of God mother." Lynne Carrow said emotionally in a heated conversation with her mother.

"Stop arguing like an illiterate person Lynne Carrow. You don't know how much your father has Faught all his life to give us this luxurious life!" Clair lashed at Lynne carrow.

"This is not the kind of life I desire mother while other citizens; People who voted for dad are suffering in various slums of our constituency." Lynne Carrow said angrily.

"leave her mother. She only pretends to be concerned about the poor." Roy said sarcastically.

Lynne Carrow looking at Roy with a sharp eye, "Yes I do care and love them unlike some other people…"

"Then if you love them go and live with them in the slums." Roy said kiddingly.

Immediately a knock was heard from the door. Roy went to check and it was their father Mr. Masur accompanied by his six body guards. He hugged his wife, kissed his children and sat next to his wife Clair.

He then showed Clair a photo of the new Lambo Guinea he had ordered for her and which was to be delivered in a week's time.

Roy woke up from where he was sited , joined them and thanked his father for buying such an expensive car for his mother.

"What about you Lynne. Don't you have anything to say about this.?" Mr. Masur looking at his daughter's eyes asked smilingly.

Lynne Carrow standing, "yes. I have something Dad ! Why do you have to buy such an expensive car for mum at this time? She already have three cars. Aren't they enough?"

"Come on sweetheart. Yours will be coming next month." He said jokingly.

"No dad. I don't need a car. Think of those people in the slums who voted for you and yet they cannot afford to educate their kids, or have proper medical care. Sometimes they cannot afford to put food on their table. Those people deserve better lives dad." She harshly responded to her greedy father.

"Forget them my dear. Their work ended at the ballot. I already paid them during the campaigns. Now it's your time. Our time to enjoy" Mr. Masur Said confidently.

"No dad. You are mistaken. You still need those people for your reelection. Over and above, they deserve to be treated with great care and concern. Don't forget that all the power belongs to the people." Lynne Carrow said as she sat back on her sit.

"Yes, I concur with you sweetheart. I need them but not now. When the right time comes, I will do my thing. Like I always do" Mr. Masur said smilingly and confidently.

Lynne Carrow looking at her father, " Dad. You mean bribing them with the money which you have already purloined from them? I will never support you in this."

She picked her cell phone from the table and headed to her bedroom. Roy followed her slowly as Clair and Masur were left in the living room.

Clair emotionally, " Your daughter can sometimes be paranoid."

"Forget her honey. She is just a child and she knows nothing about politics. Let's go and enjoy ourselves" Mr. Masur said in a jovial mood.

They held each other's hand their bedroom bound.

Smoke was all over the small wooden house. Benjamin took a spoon and put it in the pot. He removed some pieces of plain githeri to taste and it was still hard. The pot had been boiling for hours and yet the food was far from being ready. He sat down holding his head. Benjamin was troubled because Stela his young sister was starting to doze and there was no alternative meal for her. A whistle was heard from outside and they knew at once it was their father Mr. Mutinda. He entered staggering out of his drunkenness.

Esther Benjamin's mother also entered immediately after her husband. She had just closed her illicit brew stall just next to their wooden house. Benjamin had decided to serve the supper as it was, due to his young sister's fate.

Benjamin sitting on a stool at one corner of their single room, his face filled with frustration, "Dad, mom, I can't believe how blind you are to the realities of our community. How can you continue to support Mr. Masur, knowing all the harm he has caused?"

"What are you talking about, son? Mr. Masur is a good man, always taking care of his own." Mr. Mutinda stumbling into the room, slurred his words.

Benjamin with his voice filled with disappointment, "Dad, open your eyes! Have you forgotten the promises he made during his campaign? He swore to uplift our community, to provide basic amenities, and to fight for justice. But what has he done? Nothing! We still live in poverty, struggling to survive while he basks in luxury. Over and above, he is among the members of parliament pushing for salary increment. In fact, he presented the bill to the parliament"

Esther entering the room, slightly intoxicated, " Benjamin, don't disrespect your father like that. Mr. Masur has helped us in ways you can't even imagine."

"Mom, selling illicit brew to make ends meet shouldn't be our way of life. We deserve better, and it's high time we held our leaders accountable. Mr. Masur's actions only perpetuate the cycle of poverty and corruption. Can't you see that?" Benjamin said in frustration.

Mr. Mutinda defensively, "You don't understand, son. Mr. Masur provides for his family, just like your mother and I provide for ours. It's a tough world out there, and you need to learn to survive."

"Survival shouldn't come at the cost of our dignity, Dad. We deserve a leader who genuinely cares about the welfare of the people, who fights for justice, and who uplifts the marginalized. Mr. Masur has failed us, and it's time we take matters into our own hands." Benjamin said his voice filled with determination.

Esther pleadingly, " Benjamin, don't speak ill of Mr. Masur. He may not be perfect, but he has done some good things for our community."

"What has he done mom, settling for mediocrity is not the answer. We have the power to make a difference, to create real change. We can't continue to turn a blind eye to the corruption and the suffering of our neighbors. It's time we stand up, fight for what is right, and build a community that we can all be proud of." Benjamin answered passionately.

As the tension filled the room, Benjamin's words lingered in the air, challenging his parents' beliefs and igniting a spark of hope within himself. It was a difficult conversation, but one that needed to happen in order to pave the way for a new beginning, a future where the people's voices would no longer be silenced and visions of many shattered by empty promises and deceptive politicians.

Mutinda leaning heavily against the wall, his voice slurred "Benjamin, you talk of change and fighting for justice, but what do you know about the real world? We've been living in this struggle for years, and Mr. Masur has been there for us."

Benjamin frustrated, but trying to remain composed, " Dad, I understand that life has been tough for us. But we can't let that be an excuse for accepting the status quo. We have the power to rise above these circumstances, to demand better for ourselves and our community."

"Benjamin, you have good intentions, but it's not as simple as you make it sound. Mr. Masur has connections and influence that we can't even begin to comprehend. How do you expect us to fight against that?" Esther responded sighing heavily.

Benjamin passionately, "Mom, I know it won't be easy. But we can't let fear and complacency hold us back. We need to find our own strength, to unite with others who share our vision, and to challenge the corrupt system that has kept us down for far too long."

Mr. Mutinda mumbling, " It's easy for you to talk, Benjamin. You haven't seen the consequences of going against those in power. We've got to protect our own, even if it means compromising our principles."

"Dad, I refuse to accept that as our reality. We can't keep perpetuating the cycle of corruption and injustice. We owe it to ourselves and future generations to strive for a better future. I promise to fight today for a better tomorrow." Benjamin confirmed firmly.

Silence enveloped the room as the weight of their differing perspectives hung heavily in the air.

Benjamin's heart ached, knowing that his parents, whom he loved dearly, couldn't fully grasp his desire for change. But he couldn't let their fears and resignation dampen his spirit. He knew that the journey ahead would be arduous, but he was resolved to take a stand, to be a voice for those who had been silenced for far too long.

With a determined gaze, Benjamin stood up from the stool, his conviction unwavering. He knew that he would face obstacles, pushback, and perhaps even betrayal, but he was prepared to face it all. The fire within him burned brightly, fueling his resolve to fight for justice and to prove that a better future was possible, even in the face of adversity.

Little did Benjamin know that his path would soon cross with Lynne Carrow, a young woman equally passionate about bringing change to their community. Together, they would become a force to be reckoned with, challenging the very foundation of corruption and greed that had plagued their constituency for far too long.

In the sprawling city, a stark divide existed, separating the haves from the have-nots, the privileged from the oppressed. Within this intricate web of contrasts, two families stood at opposite ends of the social spectrum, their lives epitomizing the vast disparities that plagued their community.

In the heart of the city's affluent neighborhood, behind towering walls and ornate gates, at the Narek estate resided the Masur family. Mr. Masur, a powerful and influential member of parliament, reveled in the trappings of wealth and power. His opulent mansion, adorned with exquisite artwork and furnished with the finest luxuries, stood as a symbol of his elevated status. His every move was carefully orchestrated to secure his position and protect his wealth day and night, leaving little or no room for empathy or concern for those less fortunate in the community.

Clair Masur, Mr. Masur's wife, was the embodiment of extravagance and materialistic desires. She spent her days flitting from one social event to another, surrounded by a coterie of wealthy and influential acquaintances. The pursuit of luxury and pleasure consumed her, overshadowing any sense of responsibility towards the community she lived in.

Their son, Roy, grew up cocooned within a bubble of privilege, shielded from the harsh realities of the world. From a young age, he became accustomed to a life of opulence, his desires fulfilled with a mere snap of his fingers. The plight of the less fortunate remained an abstract concept, distant and inconsequential to his comfortable existence.

However, it was their eldest daughter, Lynne Carrow, who begun to question the moral compass of her family. As she matured into a young woman, she developed a deep sense of empathy and a longing for justice. Especially to the people in her constituency and the community at large. The lavish lifestyle that surrounded her felt increasingly hollow, a stark contrast to the suffering she witnessed within the confines of their constituency.

On the other side of the city, amidst the dilapidated dwellings of the Arbik slums, the Mutinda family struggled to make ends meet. Mr. Mutinda, burdened by the weight of his own demons, sought solace in the bottom of a bottle, numbing his dreams and aspirations with each passing sip. He had long abandoned his pursuit of a better life, resigned to the fate that poverty had dealt him.

Esther, his resilient wife, bore the weight of their hardships on her shoulders. In order to provide for their family, she resorted to selling illicit brew, turning a blind eye to the moral gray area in which she operated. The meager profits barely sustained them, leaving little room for dreams, visions or aspirations.

But their son, Benjamin, possessed a spirit that burned brightly against the backdrop of their circumstances. He despised the corrupt practices of politicians like Mr. Masur, who turned a blind eye to the struggles of their constituents. Benjamin yearned to be a force of change, to uplift his people from the clutches of poverty and injustice. He always dreamed of a day when he could step into the political arena and make a difference.

The divide between the Masur and Mutinda families seemed insurmountable, their values and aspirations at opposite ends of the spectrum. While the Masur's reveled in their wealth and power, the Mutinda's battled against the tides of poverty, their dreams shackled by the constraints of their circumstances. And their visions shattered by the leadership of greed and ignorance.

As the city bustled with the disparities that defined its existence, fate would soon intertwine the lives of these two families, as Lynne Carrow and Benjamin found themselves on a collision course. The meeting of their hearts and minds would ignite a spark of hope, a glimmer of possibility in the face of overwhelming odds. And from this moment of convergence, a journey would unfold, one that would test the boundaries of love, resilience, and restoration.

Chapter 2:

The Symposium

The day itself was a bit cold, at the Memorial international conference center, many schools from the city gathered that morning ready for the big debate. Different schools were matched with their opponents and presented with their respective topics and each of the candidates was ready to present their school in the best way ever.

The debate symposium buzzed with anticipation as Lynne Carrow and Benjamin prepared to engage in a passionate discussion about politics, ethics, and their visions for a better future. The room was filled with academics, activists, and community leaders, eager to witness the clash of ideas between these two formidable figures.

As the symposium commenced, Lynne and Benjamin took their places on stage, poised to share their perspectives. The moderator introduced them, acknowledging their dedication and the transformative impact they had already made on their schools. Here's the speech between Lynne Carrow and Benjamin, where they engage in a tough conversation on a key issue:

Moderator:

Our next question concerns the topic of healthcare reform. Lynne, you have advocated for a universal healthcare system, while Benjamin, you have emphasized community-driven initiatives. How do you reconcile your differing approaches in addressing the pressing healthcare needs of our constituents?

Lynne:

Thank you for the question. Healthcare is a fundamental right, and it's our duty as public servants to ensure that every individual has access to quality care, regardless of their socioeconomic status. A universal healthcare system is the most effective way to achieve this. It will remove the barriers that prevent people from seeking essential treatments, reduce healthcare disparities, and provide financial security to families in times of illness. We cannot turn a blind eye to the suffering caused by a broken system that prioritizes profits over people's well-being.

Benjamin:

I understand the importance of accessible healthcare, Lynne, but we must also acknowledge the limitations of a one-size-fits-all approach. Community-driven initiatives have the potential to address healthcare needs at the grassroots level, tailored to the specific challenges faced by each community. By empowering local clinics and healthcare professionals, we can foster innovation, promote preventive care, and ensure that healthcare solutions are responsive to the unique needs of our constituents. Let's not underestimate the power of individuals taking control of their own health.

Lynne:

Benjamin, while community-driven initiatives have their merits, they can't guarantee equitable access for all. A fragmented system leaves too many people behind, unable to afford life-saving treatments or preventive care. We need a comprehensive system that doesn't discriminate based on income or preexisting conditions. We have a responsibility to ensure that healthcare is a right, not a privilege, and that means providing universal coverage that leaves no one behind.

Benjamin:

Lynne, I agree that no one should be left behind, but we must also consider the financial implications of a universal healthcare system. It's essential to explore sustainable solutions that balance the need for coverage with fiscal responsibility. By empowering communities to take ownership of their healthcare, we can innovate, find cost-effective solutions, and ensure that resources are allocated where they are needed the most. A top-down approach might sound appealing, but it risks burdening future generations with insurmountable debt.

Lynne:

Benjamin, I understand your concern, but let's not forget that healthcare costs are already burdening individuals and families.

People shouldn't have to choose between paying their medical bills or putting food on the table. We need bold solutions that address the root causes of skyrocketing healthcare costs, such as negotiating drug prices, investing in preventive care, and implementing effective cost-control measures. A universal healthcare system is not just morally right; it is economically sensible in the long run.

Benjamin:

Lynne, I appreciate your passion for universal coverage, but we must acknowledge the potential consequences of a government-controlled healthcare system. It risks stifling innovation, limiting choices, and placing an overwhelming burden on taxpayers. Instead, let's harness the power of community-driven initiatives, partnering with healthcare providers, nonprofits, and businesses to foster a system that is responsive, sustainable, and accountable to the needs of our constituents. We can find a middle ground that combines accessibility with individual empowerment.

Moderator:

Thank you both for your insightful perspectives. It's clear that healthcare is a complex issue that requires careful consideration. Your differing approaches offer a glimpse *into the range of solutions that can*

be explored.

The room was filled with applauds as Lynne Carrow and Benjamin shook their hands while leaving the stage. From far you could tell that the debate was one of a kind.

The conversation began with probing questions about the role of government in addressing systemic inequality. Lynne, eloquent and passionate, spoke of the need for comprehensive policy reforms that would uplift marginalized communities, provide equal access to education and healthcare, and dismantle the structures of corruption that perpetuated injustice.

Benjamin, his voice filled with conviction, emphasized the importance of grassroots movements and community empowerment. He stressed the significance of local initiatives and the need for individuals to actively participate in shaping their own destinies. He proposed community-led solutions, with government serving as a facilitator rather than an omnipotent force.

As the discussion evolved, their perspectives clashed, revealing both their shared values and the nuances in their approaches. Lynne advocated for systemic change, emphasizing the role of government in creating a fair and just society. She highlighted the importance of redistributing wealth, ensuring social safety nets, and enacting policies that addressed the root causes of poverty and inequality.

Benjamin, on the other hand, emphasized the strength and resilience of communities. He believed that by fostering self-sufficiency and providing resources directly to the people, communities could rise above adversity. He emphasized the importance of education, entrepreneurship, and building networks of support within communities.

Their arguments grew more animated, with each passionately defending their positions. Yet, amidst the spirited debate, they also discovered common ground. Both Lynne and Benjamin shared a deep commitment to inclusivity, transparency, and the empowerment of marginalized voices. They recognized that collaboration between government and grassroots initiatives was crucial to achieving sustainable change.

Their conversation delved into the ethics of politics and the challenges of maintaining integrity in a system tainted by corruption. Lynne shared her experiences of navigating the temptations of power and her unwavering commitment to ethical leadership. Benjamin, drawing from his own journey, spoke of the importance of remaining true to one's values and the necessity of leading by example.

Their exchange captivated the audience, who were inspired by the authenticity and passion with which Lynne and Benjamin spoke. The symposium became a microcosm of the larger struggle for social change, a testament to the power of dialogue and the possibility of finding common ground amidst divergent perspectives.

Driven by her unwavering belief in a better future, Lynne Carrow approached Benjamin after the symposium, determined to bridge the gap that divided them. She shared her own frustrations with her father's callousness and greed, emphasizing that her beliefs and desires for change were in direct opposition to his actions. She longed for Benjamin to see her as an ally, rather than an extension of her family's corrupt legacy.

As they spoke, Benjamin couldn't help but be captivated by Lynne Carrow's sincerity and conviction. Her words resonated deeply within him, stirring a glimmer of hope that perhaps, just perhaps, there was more to her than met the eye. Slowly, the walls of skepticism began to crumble, and he allowed himself to entertain the possibility of a partnership with this woman who possessed both intelligence and compassion.

As the symposium drew to a close, Lynne and Benjamin found themselves sitting side by side, exhaustion mingling with a shared sense of purpose. They realized that while their approaches differed, their ultimate goal was the same: to create a society where every individual had the opportunity to thrive and be heard.

They agreed to continue the conversation beyond the symposium, recognizing the value of collaboration and the strength that could be found in merging their visions. Lynne and Benjamin understood that their combined efforts could forge a path forward, one that harnessed the power of government and grassroots movements in a unified pursuit of justice.

Lynne Carrow and Benjamin continued to engage in passionate discussions, challenging each other's ideas, and ultimately discovering the strength that could be found in their partnership. Their encounters would shape not only their individual journeys but also the trajectory of their shared mission to build a more equitable and compassionate society.

United by their determination, fueled by their shared values, Lynne and Benjamin set forth on a collaborative journey that would test their convictions, and challenge their assumptions.

As time went on, Lynne Carrow and Benjamin continued to engage in passionate discussions, forming a bond built on mutual respect and a shared commitment to effecting meaningful change. Their encounters became more frequent as they realized the power of their partnership in shaping their respective visions for a better future.

Lynne Carrow sat on a bench at a boarding lounge at the airport. She could not stop thinking about Benjamin and the kind of Determination he possessed for helping the people and bringing about change. But she could not help. She was already going to spent several years abroad doing her studies. It was evident that the fight which they had started together with Benjamin was going to be heavy for him alone. But Lynne Carrow knew she would support Benjamin no matter what. Still in the same thought, she received a call from Benjamin who was wishing her a safe journey and all the best in her studies endeavors. Benjamin promised her that he was going to remain strong in his stand to bring change, and Lynne Carrow promised him that she would come back to support him. Their conversation ended with tears dropping from Lynne Carrow's eyes as she bid him goodbye over the phone.

Chapter 3:

Stela's Tragedy

In the depths of the sprawling slums, tragedy struck the Mutinda family, casting a dark cloud over their hopes and dreams. Stela, the young daughter of Mr. Mutinda and Esther, became a victim of a heinous crime. It was a day that would forever change their lives.

The sun had begun its descent as Stela made her way home from school, her innocent laughter echoing through the narrow alleys. Little did she know that lurking in the shadows was a predator, waiting to shatter her world. In a moment of unspeakable horror, Stela fell victim to a violent act that left her broken and scarred. Someone abducted her and took her in a dark place behind the slums, rapped her and left her unattended. Stela lost her conscious after the heinous crime was committed on her. It wasn't until a group of other students found her dumped by the side of a river. They shouted for help and Stela was able to be rushed to the hospital.

As the devastating news reached the Mutinda household, grief washed over them like a relentless wave. Mr. Mutinda, a man known for his jovial spirit, sank into a sea of despair, his eyes filled with anguish. Esther, her heart heavy with guilt and sorrow, clung to her daughter, her tears mixing with Stela's.

Their sense of safety shattered, the Mutinda family found themselves caught in a whirlwind of emotions. Anger, fear, and an overwhelming desire for justice consumed them. They knew all too well the harsh reality that justice, especially for those without means, often came at a steep price.

With determination etched on their faces, they mustered the strength to report the crime and seek justice through the legal system. However, as they stepped into the daunting realm of the law, they were faced with a harsh reality—their lack of financial resources would hinder their pursuit of justice. Lawyers demanded exorbitant fees, leaving the Mutinda family feeling helpless and marginalized.

Days turned into weeks, and weeks into months, as their cries for justice fell on deaf ears. Frustration and despair threatened to engulf them, but the Mutinda family refused to succumb to the darkness that had befallen them. They sought solace in their community, sharing their story and rallying support from those who had also experienced the harsh realities of an unjust system.

Word spread like wildfire, and the plight of Stela and her family resonated with the hearts of many. People from all corners of the community, inspired by their resilience, rallied together, raising funds, and offering their support. It was a testament to the power of unity and the unwavering spirit of a community that refused to let justice be denied.

Through the tireless efforts of dedicated individuals and the unwavering determination of the Mutinda family, the case finally gained traction. The wheels of justice, though slow, began to turn, as the truth started to emerge from the shadows. The predator was apprehended, and a trial was set in motion.

In the courtroom, the Mutinda family sat side by side, their eyes fixed on the accused, their hearts heavy with the weight of their pain. Stela, her spirit scarred but unbroken, bravely faced her perpetrator, determined to find closure and ensure that no one else would suffer the same fate.

It was a grueling battle, as the defense attempted to undermine Stela's credibility and exploit the disparities in the justice system. But the Mutinda family, supported by their community, stood strong, their collective voice resounding with a demand for justice.

And finally, the moment arrived—a verdict that would determine the fate of the perpetrator and provide a glimmer of hope for the Mutinda family and the community at large. The courtroom fell silent as the judge delivered the sentence—a sentence that would bring a measure of closure and send a resounding message to the community.

With tears streaming down their faces, the Mutinda family embraced one another, their pain mingling with a sense of relief. They knew that their fight was far from over, but in that moment, they had achieved a small victory—a glimmer of justice in a world that often turned a blind eye to the suffering of the marginalized.

But as they exited the courtroom, their hearts heavy with the weight of the trial, they couldn't help but feel a bittersweet mix of emotions. While the verdict had brought a measure of closure, the scars that Stela carried would forever remind them of the injustice that had befallen their innocent daughter.

Days turned into weeks, and weeks into months, as the Mutinda family embarked on a journey of healing and rebuilding. The road was long and arduous, but their resilience fueled their determination to overcome the tragedy that had befallen them.

Supported by their community, they sought therapy and counseling for Stela, hoping to mend the wounds that ran deep within her fragile soul. It was a journey of patience and understanding, as they navigated the intricate layers of trauma, allowing Stela to reclaim her sense of self and find the strength to rise above her pain.

The Mutinda family also turned their tragedy into a catalyst for change. They became advocates for victims of sexual violence, shining a light on the flaws within the justice system and advocating for reforms that would protect the most vulnerable members of society. Through their relentless determination, they sought to prevent other families from enduring the same harrowing ordeal they had experienced.

Stela, once a symbol of innocence shattered, emerged as a beacon of resilience and courage. Her voice, once silenced by fear, grew louder and more resolute as she found solace in sharing her story. With each speaking engagement, each interview, she not only found healing but also inspired others to break their silence, encouraging victims to reclaim their power and fight for justice.

The Mutinda family's fight for justice became a rallying cry, igniting a spark within the community. People from all walks of life, touched by their story, joined forces to support victims, push for legal reforms, and create safe spaces where survivors could find solace and support.

The tragedy that had befallen Stela had become a catalyst for change—a catalyst that transformed a family's pain into a mission of hope and healing. Through their tireless efforts, they sought to create a society that would no longer tolerate the victimization of its most vulnerable members.

As the months turned into years, the Mutinda family's advocacy work bore fruit. Legislative changes were enacted, providing greater protection for victims of sexual violence, and resources were allocated to support survivors on their path to healing. It was a testament to the power of perseverance, community solidarity, and the unwavering determination to turn tragedy into triumph.

Though the scars of Stela's tragedy would forever remain, her family found solace in the knowledge that their fight had made a difference—a difference that would ripple through generations, shaping a future where justice and compassion prevailed.

In the depths of their pain, the Mutinda family had discovered a resilience they never knew existed. Stela's tragedy had not defined them but had instead ignited a fire within their hearts—a fire that would continue to burn brightly, fueling their pursuit of a more just and compassionate society.

Chapter 4:

Rising Entrepreneur

In the heart of the slums, amidst the crumbling infrastructure and the desperate cries for change, Benjamin embarked on a remarkable journey of entrepreneurship. With limited resources but an indomitable spirit, he set out to carve his own path to success. Benjamin wasn't able to continue with his studies after high school since his parents were not in a position to educate him further.

Driven by a burning desire to uplift his community, Benjamin identified an opportunity to create a business that would not only provide for his own livelihood but also bring economic empowerment to those around him. Armed with a vision and an unwavering determination, he started small—a humble stall in a bustling marketplace.

His business venture began with meager supplies, but Benjamin's resourcefulness shone through as he carefully selected products that catered to the needs of the community. With each passing day, his stall became a beacon of hope, offering essential goods and services that were previously inaccessible to many.

Word of Benjamin's enterprise spread like wildfire through the slums. The community embraced his business with open arms, recognizing that his success meant their own prosperity. Benjamin's commitment to fair pricing and quality products earned him the trust and loyalty of his customers.

But success did not come without its fair share of challenges. Benjamin faced numerous obstacles along the way—financial constraints, bureaucratic hurdles, and the ever-looming shadow of corruption that threatened to undermine his efforts. Yet, he remained steadfast, fueled by a burning determination to overcome every setback that stood in his path.

Through sheer grit and hard work, Benjamin transformed his small stall into a thriving enterprise. He expanded his offerings, diversifying into new products and services that catered to the evolving needs of his community. With each expansion, he created job opportunities, empowering individuals who had previously struggled to find employment.

Benjamin's success story resonated far beyond the boundaries of the slums. His entrepreneurial spirit and unwavering dedication inspired others to believe in their own potential. As the community witnessed the transformation happening before their eyes, a renewed sense of hope filled the air, and the belief that they too could rise above their circumstances took root

But Benjamin's journey was not just about personal gain. He reinvested a portion of his profits back into the community, initiating social initiatives that aimed to uplift the lives of the less fortunate. From funding scholarships for deserving students to organizing skill-building workshops and community development projects, Benjamin's impact extended far beyond the realm of business.

As his enterprise thrived, Benjamin became a role model—a beacon of hope for aspiring entrepreneurs who dared to dream of a better future. He shared his knowledge and experiences, mentoring young minds and guiding them along the path of success. Through his actions, he demonstrated that entrepreneurship could be a catalyst for positive change, an instrument to break free from the shackles of poverty and inequality.

But amidst his journey to uplift the community, Benjamin never lost sight of his ultimate goal—to bring lasting change to the political landscape. He knew that true transformation required not only economic empowerment but also a shift in the power dynamics that perpetuated corruption and neglect.

With his business as a platform for connection and influence, Benjamin used his growing network and resources to rally support for his political aspirations. He engaged with community leaders, organized town hall meetings, and listened to the concerns of the people, understanding that their voices were the driving force behind the change they sought.

As Benjamin's influence and impact expanded, so did his determination to challenge the very system that had allowed corruption to thrive. He recognized that his entrepreneurial journey was intrinsically linked to his political aspirations—they were two sides of the same coin, both driven by his unwavering commitment to making a difference.

Reality marked a significant turning point in Benjamin's life—a testament to his resourcefulness, resilience, and unyielding determination. As he continued to rise as an entrepreneur, his vision for a better community burned brighter than ever. Benjamin's success as an entrepreneur not only transformed his own life but also served as a powerful example for others to follow. The slums, once plagued by despair and hopelessness, now brimmed with renewed energy and aspirations.

Recognizing the need for sustainable development, Benjamin embraced innovative approaches to address pressing social and environmental challenges. He spearheaded initiatives that promoted eco-friendly practices, such as waste management and renewable energy solutions. By empowering the community with knowledge and resources, he fostered a sense of environmental consciousness and responsibility.

Moreover, Benjamin's business acumen and dedication to social impact attracted the attention of investors and philanthropists who shared his vision. They recognized the transformative potential of his entrepreneurial endeavors and offered support in the form of funding, mentorship, and partnerships. This newfound collaboration allowed Benjamin to scale his business and expand its reach, amplifying the positive impact he was making on the community.

As his influence grew, Benjamin leveraged his position to advocate for policy changes that would benefit not only his own business but also the wider entrepreneurial ecosystem. He passionately advocated for fair regulations, access to financing, and supportive infrastructure, ensuring that aspiring entrepreneurs faced fewer barriers on their own journeys to success.

But Benjamin's success as an entrepreneur did not come without sacrifices. The long hours, sleepless nights, and the weight of responsibility took their toll.

There were moments of self-doubt when he questioned whether he had the strength to continue. Yet, the unwavering support of his loved ones and the profound impact he witnessed in the lives of those around him fueled his determination to push forward.

In the midst of his entrepreneurial pursuits, Benjamin remained rooted in his political aspirations. He recognized that true systemic change required not only economic empowerment but also a seat at the table where decisions were made. With his growing influence and the trust he had earned from the community, Benjamin embarked on a shadow campaign for public office.

The slums, once skeptical of politicians, rallied behind Benjamin, inspired by his integrity, resilience, and demonstrated commitment to their well-being. His entrepreneurial journey had instilled a sense of hope, reminding the community that they were not powerless, that their dreams were within reach.

Benjamin's voice reverberated through the slums and beyond. He eloquently articulated his vision for a constituency where every voice was heard, where corruption had no place, and where the dreams of its residents could be realized. His authenticity and passion struck a chord with voters, who yearned for a leader who understood their struggles and genuinely fought for their rights.

This was a beginning of a new chapter in Benjamin's life—a chapter where his entrepreneurial success intersected with his political aspirations. The boundaries between the two blurred as he harnessed the power of entrepreneurship to drive his political agenda, creating a synergy that magnified his impact on the community.

The road ahead was challenging, with obstacles and opposition awaiting him at every turn. But Benjamin's journey as an entrepreneur had taught him resilience, adaptability, and the ability to find innovative solutions to complex problems. He was prepared to confront the power structures that perpetuated inequality, to challenge the status quo, and to advocate for a constituency where everyone had an equal opportunity to thrive.

As time went on, the stage was set for Benjamin's dual roles as a rising entrepreneur and a political force to be reckoned with. The slums had witnessed the power of one individual's determination to bring about change, and they stood united in their support for Benjamin's unwavering pursuit of a better future.

The story of Benjamin's rise as an entrepreneur and his unwavering commitment to his community would continue to unfold, intertwining with the lives of those he touched along the way. The journey was far from over.

Chapter 5:

Benjamin's Determination

From a young age, Benjamin had witnessed the hardships endured by his community. Poverty, corruption, and a lack of opportunities were the pervasive realities that shaped his upbringing. But instead of succumbing to despair, Benjamin chose a different path—one that would allow him to make a difference in the lives of those around him.

Benjamin's dream of becoming a politician took root early on, fueled by an unyielding determination to challenge the systemic injustices that held his community captive. He recognized that the power to effect change lay not only in the hands of the privileged but also in the hands of those who understood the struggles firsthand.

Born into humble circumstances, Benjamin faced numerous obstacles on his journey to realizing his aspirations. Limited access to quality education and the absence of influential connections were hurdles he had to overcome. But these challenges only steeled his resolve, fueling his hunger for knowledge and propelling him to carve his own path.

With unwavering determination, Benjamin sought out every opportunity to educate himself and develop the skills necessary to navigate the complex world of politics. He devoured books on leadership, policy, and governance, absorbing knowledge like a sponge. He sought mentors among the few who had managed to break free from the cycle of poverty, learning from their experiences and drawing inspiration from their resilience.

Despite facing skepticism and derision from some who doubted his ability to succeed, Benjamin refused to be discouraged. He understood that his background, far from being a limitation, was a source of strength—a lens through which he could view the struggles of his community with a level of empathy and understanding that the privileged could never fully grasp.

Benjamin embraced his role as a voice for the voiceless, an advocate for those whose pleas had long fallen on deaf ears. He immersed himself in community work, dedicating countless hours to organizing grassroots initiatives and championing causes that were close to his heart. He rallied his neighbors, igniting a spark of hope and inspiring them to believe in the power of collective action.

The road was not easy. Benjamin encountered resistance from those who sought to maintain the status quo, to perpetuate the very systems of oppression that he fought against. He faced threats and intimidation, his resolve tested at every turn. But he stood tall, refusing to be silenced by fear.

Benjamin's determination was fortified by the support of like-minded individuals who shared his vision for a better future. Together, they formed a tight-knit network, leveraging their collective strengths to challenge the corrupt powers that had long held their community hostage. Through collaboration and strategic alliances, they devised innovative solutions to address the deep-rooted issues plaguing their constituency.

As Benjamin's influence grew, so did the hope within the hearts of the people he hoped to represent. His unwavering commitment and ability to connect with individuals on a personal level earned him their trust and respect. He listened to their stories, their aspirations, and their grievances, ensuring that their voices were heard and their concerns were addressed.

Benjamin's resilience and determination shone through in the face of adversity. Each setback only fueled his hunger for change, propelling him to work harder, to think more creatively, and to push the boundaries of what was deemed possible. He refused to be confined by the limitations imposed upon him by his background, instead using them as stepping stones to ascend to greater heights.

As time flew, Benjamin stood at the precipice of a new phase in his journey. The upcoming election would serve as the ultimate test of his determination, a battleground where he would face off against powerful incumbents and a deeply entrenched system. But Benjamin was undeterred, armed with a fierce belief in his ability to bring about meaningful change.

Benjamin's resilience and unwavering determination would be put to the test as he prepared to embark on a campaign trail that would define his political career.

Benjamin understood that his journey was not just about personal ambition; it was about lifting his community out of the shadows of neglect and despair. He developed a comprehensive platform that addressed the pressing issues faced by his constituents—education reform, job creation, healthcare access, and the eradication of corruption. With each policy proposal, he aimed to build a foundation for a more equitable society, one that valued the inherent worth and potential of every individual.

 Benjamin traversed neighborhoods and villages, engaging directly with the people he sought to represent. He listened intently to their stories, their dreams, and their concerns. He spoke passionately, articulating a vision of hope and progress that resonated deeply within the hearts of his audience.

His rallies were characterized by an electrifying energy, as the disenfranchised found solace and inspiration in Benjamin's unwavering dedication. His ability to connect with people on a personal level, to empathize with their struggles, and to offer tangible solutions set him apart from the political elite who had long been disconnected from the realities of everyday life.

Despite facing well-funded opponents and a political machinery that seemed insurmountable, Benjamin refused to be intimidated. He relied on his tireless work ethic, his extensive knowledge of the issues, and the unwavering support of a dedicated team of volunteers. Together, they knocked on doors, held community forums, and organized grassroots events that galvanized support for their cause.

Throughout the grueling adventures, Benjamin's determination remained unshakable. He confronted smear threats, malicious rumors, and attempts to undermine his credibility. But he faced each challenge head-on, armed with integrity and an unyielding belief in the power of truth.

Benjamin's personal story resonated deeply with the constituents he sought to serve. His journey from humble beginnings to the doorstep of political leadership symbolized the possibilities that could be achieved through resilience and determination. He became a beacon of hope, a symbol of what was possible when an individual was driven by a genuine desire to effect positive change.

Chapter 6:

The Power of Corruption

In the heart of the constituency, a web of corruption ensnared the political landscape, with Mr. Masur at its center. Behind the charismatic facade, he operated with impunity, using his position of power to amass personal wealth and influence while the citizens he was meant to serve languished in poverty.

Under the guise of public service, Mr. Masur manipulated the system to his advantage. He siphoned off funds meant for essential development projects, diverting them into his own pockets and those of his cronies. Schools remained dilapidated, healthcare facilities were woefully inadequate, and infrastructure crumbled, all while Mr. Masur reveled in the opulence of his ill-gotten wealth.

Bribery became his modus operandi, as he shamelessly bought the loyalty of citizens with meager sums during election seasons. The impoverished electorate, desperate for immediate relief, succumbed to his manipulative tactics, unaware of the long-term repercussions of their complicity.

The constituency fund, intended to uplift the lives of the people, became a bottomless pit from which Mr. Masur drew without remorse. He cunningly diverted funds into his own businesses and those of his family, forging lucrative deals that further enriched his already overflowing coffers. While he and his family lived in extravagant mansions, the majority of his constituents barely scraped by, trapped in a cycle of poverty that seemed inescapable.

To maintain his stranglehold on power, Mr. Masur employed a network of loyal enforcers who ensured his opponents faced relentless harassment and intimidation. Journalists who dared to expose his corrupt practices found themselves silenced, their voices stifled under the weight of threats and coercion.

But the darkness of Mr. Masur's corruption did not go unnoticed. Whispers of dissent grew louder, spreading like wildfire through the constituency. There were brave souls who saw through his deceit, individuals who yearned for a leader who would prioritize their well-being over personal gain.

Among those who dared to challenge Mr. Masur was Benjamin, driven by a fierce determination to break the chains of corruption that bound their community. With each passing day, his resolve grew stronger, his desire to bring justice and equality burning brightly within him.

As Benjamin's popularity swelled, Mr. Masur recognized the threat posed by this young upstart. He unleashed a wave of defamation and smear campaigns, hoping to tarnish Benjamin's reputation and maintain his grip on power. Yet, Benjamin remained steadfast, his integrity untarnished by the dirty tricks employed against him.

The battle for the soul of the constituency intensified day after the other. Benjamin and his supporters mobilized, emboldened by a shared vision of a better future, free from the clutches of corruption. They knocked on doors, held rallies, and engaged in grassroots organizing, spreading the message of change and inspiring hope in the hearts of the weary.

The contrast between Benjamin's integrity and Mr. Masur's corruption became starkly apparent. The citizens, once lured by empty promises and temporary handouts, began to see through the facade of their incumbent representative. They yearned for a leader who would prioritize their needs, address their grievances, and work tirelessly for the betterment of all.

Chapter 7:

Forbidden Love

The motor cade ran through the express way down to the streets of Nerak Estate. Stirring amidst the affluent neighborhood, nestled behind high walls and ornate gates, Lynne Carrow was back home. Dignitaries from the political divide and big fishes of the business fraternity were present. The home coming Party of one Lynne Carrow was a posh one. The buffet contained all types of food and the taproom contained all sorts of Drinks. Every one within the party was happy and enjoying.

But for Lynne carrow who had spent over three years away from home, didn't seem as happy as everyone expected. She still had a lot to catch up with perhaps to pick from where she had left. Again when she looked around, she only saw her father's corrupt web of cartels. She thought may be her father would change for the good of his constituents. At that moment she thought of Benjamin and the Marginalized people in the slums. She got worked up, excused herself and went to her bedroom.

Lynne Carrow found herself caught in a whirlwind of emotions as her feelings for Benjamin grew stronger. She admired his determination, his unwavering commitment to the community, and the fire in his eyes when he spoke about his vision for a better future three years back. However, Lynne faced a daunting task — convincing Benjamin that she was different from her father, that her intentions were pure, and that she genuinely wanted to make a difference in their community.

One evening, as the sun cast a warm glow over the city, Lynne mustered the courage to invite Benjamin for a walk along the riverbank within the vicinity of her opulent home in Narek estate. Mr. Masur and Clair had jetted out of the country for a week's holiday and so the time was apt for her to invite Benjamin in their homestead. She wanted to catch up with him once again and get to know the far he had gone with his campaign. Benjamin was hesitant at first but Lynne Carrow assured him that her motive was good. So Benjamin accepted the invitation and showed up that day.

As they strolled side by side, the air was thick with anticipation. Lynne searched for the right words, knowing that she had to bridge the gap between their hearts and overcome the shadow cast by her father's actions.

Finally, unable to contain her feelings any longer, Lynne took a deep breath and spoke softly, "Benjamin, I need you to understand that I am not my father. I see the suffering in our community, the injustice, and it breaks my heart. I may come from privilege, but I am determined to use that privilege to create a better future for everyone, regardless of their background."

Benjamin, his gaze fixed on the flowing river, remained silent for a moment, grappling with his own doubts and fears. "Lynne," he replied, his voice tinged with skepticism, "I have seen politicians make promises before, only to forget about them once they are in power. How can I trust that you are different?"

Lynne reached out and gently placed her hand on Benjamin's arm, trying to convey her sincerity through touch. "Benjamin, I understand your skepticism. But I ask you to look into my eyes and see the fire that burns within me. I am willing to fight tooth and nail for the change we both believe in. I am committed to transparency, accountability, and never losing sight of the people in our community. I want to be a complete partner in your mission, not a hindrance."

Benjamin turned to face Lynne, his eyes searching hers for any sign of deceit. He saw a flicker of vulnerability, a genuine desire to bridge the divide that separated them. "Lynne," he said, his voice softer now, "I want to believe you. I want to believe that love can coexist with our shared purpose. But my heart has been wounded before, and I fear the consequences of falling for someone entrenched in the world of politics."

Lynne took a step closer, her voice filled with conviction. "Benjamin, I understand your fears, and I respect them. But love can be a powerful force, one that fuels our determination and strengthens our resolve. Together, we can create a synergy, a partnership built on trust, love, and a shared vision for our community. I am ready to face the challenges ahead, hand in hand with you. I will support you in lock, stock, and barrel."

A mixture of hope and doubt flickered across Benjamin's face. He reached out, intertwining his fingers with Lynne's, as if seeking reassurance in their connection. "Lynne," he said, his voice tinged with a newfound vulnerability, "if we embark on this journey together, we must promise to hold each other accountable, to never lose sight of our purpose, and to remain true to the values we hold dear. Remember we once did before you left to further your studies. Can you promise me that?"

Lynne nodded, her heart pounding with a renewed sense of purpose. "Benjamin, I promise you that I will never forget the suffering we have witnessed, the injustices we seek to rectify. I promise to be your ally, your confidante, and your unwavering supporter. Let our love be the catalyst for change, embracing the power of unity and shared purpose. Together, Lynne and Benjamin forged a pact—a pact not just of love, but also of unwavering commitment to their community and the values they held dear.

As their forbidden love blossomed, they became a formidable force, fueled by their shared determination to break the cycle of political apathy and corruption. They embarked on a journey, hand in hand, navigating the treacherous landscape of politics while staying true to their principles.

Their love became a source of strength, empowering them to overcome the challenges that lay ahead. They faced skeptics and critics who questioned their motives and whispered doubts about their relationship. But Lynne and Benjamin remained resolute, steadfast in their belief that love and passion for the greater good could transcend any obstacle.

Together, they attended countless community gatherings, engaging with citizens from all walks of life. Lynne, armed with her eloquence and charisma, and Benjamin, with his genuine empathy and relatability, captured the hearts and minds of the people. They listened intently to the struggles and dreams of the constituents, weaving their collective voices into their political agenda.

As the campaign trail heated up, Lynne and Benjamin found themselves in the throes of a fierce battle against Lynne's own father, Mr. Masur. It was a clash between entrenched corruption and a new wave of hope. The campaign was marred by smear tactics, false accusations, and an uphill battle against the deeply ingrained systems of bribery and political manipulation.

Yet, Lynne and Benjamin remained undeterred. They crisscrossed the constituency, rallying supporters, and sharing their vision for change. Their love created a very strong bond and acted as a catalyst to their agenda.

Chapter 8:

Lynne's Awakening

In the wake of her encounters with Benjamin and their shared discussions on the plight of their constituency, a transformation began to take hold within Lynne Carrow. Seeds of doubt and empathy sprouted, intertwining with her existing discontent, and igniting a burning desire for change.

As Lynne Carrow delved deeper into her father's political dealings, she discovered a web of corruption that ran far deeper than she had ever imagined. The scales fell from her eyes, revealing the extent to which the Masur family had exploited their power, perpetuating the suffering of the very people they were entrusted to serve.

Lynne Carrow could no longer ignore the cries of the marginalized and oppressed, their voices echoing through her mind. She began to see the true impact of her family's actions, the lives shattered and dreams crushed under the weight of corruption and indifference. Her heart ached for the countless individuals whose struggles were dismissed, whose aspirations were smothered by a system that thrived on their despair.

Haunted by the stark contrast between her privileged upbringing and the stark realities faced by her constituency, Lynne Carrow found herself at a crossroads. The chasm between her personal drive and her family's legacy had become too vast to ignore. She yearned to break free from the shackles of her upbringing, to defy the expectations placed upon her, and to forge a path of integrity and justice.

Her partnership with Benjamin soon extended beyond political debates and public appearances. They found solace in their shared dedication to their constituency, often engaging in late-night conversations to brainstorm strategies and analyze the intricacies of governance. Their discussions delved into the complexities of social justice, economic empowerment, and the delicate balance between personal ambition and public service.

As Lynne and Benjamin continued to collaborate, their perspectives evolved and merged. Lynne's commitment to systemic change began to incorporate the importance of community-driven initiatives, while Benjamin recognized the need for policies that addressed structural inequalities. They challenged each other's assumptions, pushing the boundaries of their own understanding, and embracing the transformative power of collaboration.

Chapter 9:

Battle Ground

The stage was set for Benjamin's official political campaign, as he took his first steps towards challenging the corrupt network that had plagued their community for far too long. However, the path ahead was riddled with challenges, as he faced a formidable opponent in Mr. Masur's deeply entrenched network of corruption.

Benjamin's decision to challenge Mr. Masur's legacy was met with disbelief and skepticism from those who had witnessed the web of deceit and broken promises woven by the ruling elite. Many warned him of the consequences of going against Mr. Masur, cautioning him about the power and influence he wielded over the constituency.

Undeterred by the warnings, Benjamin relied on the unwavering support of the community members who had come to believe in his vision for a better future. Ordinary citizens, who had been marginalized and forgotten for too long, saw in Benjamin a glimmer of hope—a chance for their voices to be heard and their grievances addressed.

As Benjamin and Lynne Carrow embarked on his campaign trail, he witnessed firsthand the power of unity and collective action. The community rallied behind him, organizing rallies, door-to-door campaigns, and engaging in thought-provoking discussions about the urgent need for change. The stories of hardship, poverty, and inequality poured forth, fueling Benjamin's determination to fight for their rights and restore dignity to their lives.

The battle was not merely about winning an election; it was a fight to dismantle the web of corruption that had ensnared their community. Benjamin's message resonated with the citizens, as he vowed to be a leader who would prioritize the needs of the people over personal gain. He emphasized transparency, accountability, and the importance of involving the community in decision-making processes.

However, the fight against corruption was not without its consequences. Benjamin faced threats, intimidation, and attempts to discredit his reputation. The powers that be sought to undermine his credibility, using every trick in the book to tarnish his image and discourage the community from supporting him. But with each obstacle, Benjamin's resolve only grew stronger, fueled by the unwavering support of Lynne Carrow and those who had been yearning for change.

Tension and anticipation filled the air as Benjamin's campaign gained momentum. The battle lines were drawn, and the clash between the forces of corruption and the hopes of the community became increasingly evident.

As the campaign intensified, the community's voice grew louder, challenging the status quo and demanding accountability. Benjamin's rallying cry for justice, progress, and equal opportunities resonated deeply, inspiring even the most skeptical citizens to believe in the possibility of a brighter future.

Benjamin's journey was fraught with peril, but his unwavering spirit and the collective strength of the community propelled him forward. The outcome of this battle would shape the destiny of their constituency and determine whether their dreams of a corruption-free, inclusive society would become a reality.

Benjamin's mettle was tested, and the true power of the people was unleashed. It was a battle that would not only redefine their community but would also serve as a potent reminder of the strength and resilience that lies within every individual to challenge the forces of corruption and fight for a better tomorrow.

As Benjamin's campaign gained momentum day after the other, the battle against corruption intensified. The forces aligned against him became more desperate, resorting to underhanded tactics to undermine his credibility and discourage the community from supporting his cause.

False rumors and slanderous accusations were spread with the intention of tarnishing Benjamin's image. The corrupt network exploited their control over the media, manipulating public opinion through a barrage of negative stories. But Benjamin refused to be deterred, knowing that the truth would prevail in the end.

In the face of adversity, Benjamin's supporters rallied around him with unwavering loyalty. Community leaders, the clergy, activists, and individuals tired of being neglected by their elected representatives joined forces, forming a formidable grassroots movement. Their shared determination and passion created a sense of unity that transcended social, economic, and ethnic divisions.

The battle for hearts and minds was fought on multiple fronts. Benjamin's campaign team utilized social media platforms, organized town hall meetings, and went door-to-door, engaging directly with voters to counter the false narratives and present their vision for a better future. They highlighted Benjamin's track record of success as an entrepreneur and emphasized his commitment to transparency and accountability.

In every corner of the constituency, Benjamin's message resonated. The community members, who had long suffered the consequences of corrupt practices, saw in him a beacon of hope. They were tired of empty promises and token gestures made during election seasons. Benjamin's genuine concern for their well-being and his determination to address the issues that mattered most to them struck a chord.

As the campaign gained momentum, Lynne Carrow's father, Mr. Masur, became increasingly unnerved by his daughter's support for Benjamin and his growing popularity. The once-unbreakable bond between father and daughter was strained, replaced by a bitter rivalry fueled by divergent values and aspirations. Mr. Masur saw Benjamin's challenge as a threat to his power and the comfortable life he had built for himself and his family.

The battle between father and daughter represented a clash of ideologies—a clash between a legacy of corruption and the promise of a new era. The community watched with bated breath, their hope riding on Benjamin's ability to topple the entrenched system and usher in a period of genuine progress and representation.

The battleground remained set and firm, the lines were clearly drawn, and the community's support was firmly behind Benjamin. The battle against corruption had reached a tipping point, and the campaigns ahead would determine whether Benjamin's determination, integrity, and the collective power of the community would be enough to dismantle the stronghold of corruption and pave the way for a brighter future.

Alliances were tested, secrets were uncovered, and sacrifices were made. The battle for justice and equality came to a head, leaving an indelible mark on the lives of those involved and shaping the destiny of the community forever.

Chapter 10:

Clash of Ideals

The meeting between Lynne Carrow and her father, Mr. Masur, was charged with tension and unspoken truths. Lynne had mustered the courage to confront him, to hold him accountable for his actions and the pain he had inflicted upon their community. She knew that this confrontation would mark a turning point, not only in her relationship with her father but also in her own journey towards justice.

As Lynne entered her father's lavish study, adorned with expensive furnishings and symbols of power, her heart pounded with a mix of determination and trepidation. She found Mr. Masur seated behind his imposing desk, his face etched with a combination of surprise and wariness at her unexpected visit.

"Father," Lynne began, her voice steady but laced with an undercurrent of sadness, "we need to talk."

Mr. Masur's eyes narrowed, but he gestured for her to continue. Lynne took a deep breath, gathering her thoughts before she spoke the words that had been burning within her.

"I've seen the evidence, Father. The documents, the bank statements—it's all there. The embezzlement, the misuse of funds meant to uplift our constituency," she said, her voice trembling with a mix of disappointment and anger.

Mr. Masur's expression hardened, and he leaned back in his chair, attempting to maintain an air of nonchalance. "Lynne, you don't understand the pressures of politics. Sometimes sacrifices must be made for the greater good."

"The greater good?" Lynne retorted, her voice rising in frustration. "What about the people, Father? The ones who believed in you, who entrusted you with their hopes and dreams? You've betrayed them."

A flicker of guilt crossed Mr. Masur's face, but it quickly dissipated, replaced by a mask of indifference. "Politics is a game, my dear. And in this game, one must play to win."

Lynne's eyes welled up with tears, a mix of sorrow and resolve. "But at what cost, Father? At the cost of human lives, of children without education, families starving with hunger and without healthcare? Is that the legacy you want to leave behind?"

Mr. Masur's facade cracked momentarily, a hint of regret shining through. "You don't understand the pressures, Lynne. The compromises I had to make for our family's security and future."

Lynne shook her head, her voice now filled with determination. "There is no excuse, Father. We can't turn a blind eye to the suffering of our people, to their cries for help. It's time for change."

The room fell silent, the weight of their conversation hanging heavily in the air. In that moment, Lynne realized that she had a choice to make—a choice between loyalty to her family and her own moral compass. It was a choice that would define her, not just as an individual, but as a catalyst for transformation.

With tears streaming down her face, Lynne turned and walked toward the door, her voice choked with emotion. "I can't condone your actions, Father. I won't be a part of this corruption any longer."

As Lynne left the study, she knew that her relationship with her father would never be the same. But she also felt a newfound sense of purpose, a determination to stand against the very forces that had kept their community in chains for far too long.

Lynne stood outside her father's study; her heart heavy but resolute. The clash of ideals had set her on a path divergent from her family's legacy. She had chosen to align herself with truth, justice, and the fight for a better future. The subsequent realities would witness Lynne's unwavering commitment to her newfound cause, as she joined forces with Benjamin in their shared pursuit of justice and change.

As Lynne walked away from her father's study, the weight of her decision settled upon her shoulders. She knew that breaking away from her family's legacy of corruption and greed would come at a price. There would be personal sacrifices, fractured relationships, and a constant battle against the forces that sought to maintain the status quo.

But Lynne also felt a renewed sense of purpose, a fire burning within her to right the wrongs and restore hope to their constituency. She knew that her journey would be difficult, that the path she had chosen would be fraught with challenges, but she was determined to forge ahead.

She sought solace in the knowledge that she was not alone in her quest. Benjamin and the community stood beside her, Benjamin's unwavering support bolstering her resolve. Together, they would challenge the system, expose the depth of corruption, and rally the community behind their cause.

In the subsequent realities, Lynne and Benjamin would embark on a relentless campaign to raise awareness, mobilize support, and gather evidence against the corrupt practices plaguing their constituency. They would face threats, intimidation, and smear campaigns orchestrated by those desperate to cling to power.

But with every obstacle they encountered, Benjamin's determination grew stronger. He refused to be silenced or swayed by the manipulation and deceit that had plagued their community for far too long. He knew that the truth had the power to break through the darkness and ignite a spark of hope in the hearts of the people.

Lynne stood at the precipice of a daunting yet transformative journey. The clash of ideals with her father had marked a turning point, and she had chosen the path less traveled—a path that demanded courage, resilience, and unwavering conviction. A path of transformative leadership through Benjamin.

The battle for justice was far from over, but Benjamin and Lynne Carrow were prepared to fight with every ounce of their being. With each step forward, they would draw closer to the truth, closer to the change they sought to bring to their constituency.

The subsequent realities would reveal the immense challenges they faced, the alliances they formed, and the sacrifices they made. It would be a testament to the power of individuals who dared to challenge the corrupt establishment and restore the voice and dignity of the people they sought to represent.

Chapter 11:

Unveiling the Truth

Reality revealed the pivotal moment when Lynne Carrow stumbled upon a hidden truth that would shake the very foundations of her family and the community at large. As she delved deeper into her father's affairs, her suspicions grew, and she became determined to uncover the extent of his embezzlement.

Late nights spent poring over financial records and following trails of suspicious transactions led Lynne to irrefutable evidence of her father's corrupt practices. Shocked and disillusioned, she realized the magnitude of the betrayal her father had perpetrated against the very people he had sworn to serve.

With a heavy heart, Lynne made the difficult decision to expose her father's wrongdoings to the public. She understood that the truth had the power to ignite a fire within the community, fueling their support for Benjamin's campaign and solidifying their determination to rid their constituency of corruption once and for all.

As news of the revelation spread, the community was overcome with a mix of disbelief, anger, and a renewed sense of purpose. Lynne's courage to stand against her own family and fight for justice resonated deeply with the citizens, who had suffered under the weight of their elected officials' greed for far too long.

The revelation unleashed a storm of emotions, as citizens realized the extent of the deception and betrayal they had endured. They saw their hopes and dreams crushed by the very person they had entrusted with their future. The outrage that simmered beneath the surface now erupted into a fervor for change—a collective demand for a new era of integrity, transparency, and accountability.

The community, already mobilized by Benjamin's campaign, rallied around the truth revealed by Lynne. Benjamin's message, backed by the evidence of corruption within the ruling elite, gained even greater momentum. The citizens, driven by a newfound determination, vowed to cast their votes against the forces that had neglected and exploited them.

In the wake of the revelation, Benjamin and Lynne formed an unbreakable alliance. They stood united in their mission to bring justice to their community, to restore dignity to the lives of the marginalized, and to ensure that those who had abused their power were held accountable.

Reality revealed the community embracing truth and rallying behind Benjamin's campaign with unwavering support. The battle against corruption had reached a turning point, and the journey ahead promised to be filled with both triumphs and challenges. The subsequent realities would witness the community's collective strength as they marched forward, undeterred by the obstacles that lay in their path, fueled by the desire to reclaim their constituency from the grip of corruption and build a brighter future for generations to come.

Alliances would be forged, alliances would crumble, and the fight for justice and equality would escalate. The story would unfold as Benjamin and Lynne confronted their adversaries head-on, leaving an indelible mark on their community and inspiring a generation to rise up against the forces of greed and indifference.

As the news of Lynne Carrow's revelation spread like wildfire through the community, a wave of shock and disbelief washed over the constituency. The citizens grappled with the harsh reality that their trusted representative, Mr. Masur, had been embezzling funds meant for their welfare and development.

The evidence presented by Lynne was undeniable. Documents, bank statements, and testimonies painted a damning picture of her father's corrupt practices. The community members, who had long suspected foul play but lacked concrete proof, were both outraged and relieved to have their suspicions confirmed.

The revelation struck a deep chord within the hearts of the citizens. It was a shutter of their visions, betrayal of their trust, a betrayal of their hopes for a better future. Their anger simmered, fueled by years of neglect and broken promises. The once-silent majority found their voice, their frustration giving way to a collective determination to take a stand against the prevailing culture of corruption.

Benjamin's campaign, already gaining momentum, received an unprecedented surge of support. The community, now armed with the knowledge of their incumbent representative's misdeeds, rallied behind Benjamin's call for change. They saw in him not just a political contender, but a symbol of integrity, honesty, and a genuine commitment to their well-being.

Town hall meetings and rallies took on a new fervor, as citizens passionately shared their stories of struggle, exploitation, and the urgent need for a leader who would prioritize their needs. The revelation acted as a catalyst, uniting the community in a shared purpose— to reclaim their constituency from the clutches of corruption and restore dignity to their lives.

Lynne, burdened by the weight of her father's transgressions, became a beacon of courage and integrity. She was determined to make amends, to atone for her family's sins, and to stand alongside Benjamin as they fought for justice. Their bond grew stronger, forged in the crucible of truth and a shared vision for a better future.

The battle against corruption intensified, as Benjamin and Lynne led the charge to expose the extent of the corrupt practices that had plagued their community. They assembled a team of dedicated volunteers, lawyers, and activists who worked tirelessly to compile evidence, engage the media, and bring public attention to the pervasive issue.

As the campaign gained traction, the ruling elite grew increasingly desperate. They attempted to discredit Benjamin and undermine the validity of the evidence. Rumors were spread, threats were made, and attempts to buy the loyalty of the community were carried out behind closed doors. But the community, armed with the truth, remained resolute in their support for Benjamin and their rejection of the corrupt status quo.

Reality revealed the community standing united, ready to cast their votes as a powerful voice against corruption. The battle had shifted from an individual's quest for political office to a collective fight for justice and accountability. The subsequent realities would see the culmination of their efforts, as they navigated through the intricate web of political intrigue, faced personal sacrifices, and tested the limits of their determination to bring about lasting change.

Forging ahead, the battle would reach its climax, and the destinies of the characters would intertwine with the fate of their constituency. Benjamin and Lynne would face their greatest challenges yet, but their unwavering resolve and the unwavering support of the community would propel them forward. Together, they would strive to ensure that the truth remained unveiled, justice prevailed, and a brighter, more equitable future awaited their constituency.

The revelation of Mr. Masur's corruption sent shockwaves throughout the community, igniting a fervor for change and justice. As the news spread, citizens from all walks of life gathered in town squares and community centers, their anger palpable, their demand for accountability echoing through the streets.

Lynne Carrow, burdened by the weight of her father's misdeeds, knew that she had a duty to ensure the truth reached every corner of their constituency. With unwavering determination, she took to the airwaves, appearing on radio shows and television interviews, exposing the intricate web of corruption that had ensnared her father and tainted their community.

Her voice trembled with a mix of sorrow and determination as she recounted the stories of struggling families, schools in disrepair, and hospitals lacking basic medical supplies—all while her father had enriched himself at the expense of those he was elected to serve. The citizens listened intently; their hearts heavy with the realization that their suffering was not merely a result of circumstance but of a systematic betrayal of trust.

Benjamin stood by Lynne's side throughout the media blitz, his presence a testament to their shared vision for a better future. He, too, had witnessed firsthand the consequences of Mr. Masur's greed. The slums where he had grown up, the struggles of his family and neighbors—these were the fuel that propelled his fight against corruption.

Together, Benjamin and Lynne forged ahead, undeterred by the backlash they faced from Mr. Masur's supporters. They faced smear campaigns, threats, and attempts to discredit their credibility. But the truth, now out in the open, resonated deeply with the citizens. The community rallied behind Benjamin, recognizing him as a beacon of hope amidst the darkness of corruption.

As the battle lines were drawn, Benjamin's campaign gained momentum. Volunteers flooded their headquarters, offering their time, skills, and resources to support the cause. The once-disillusioned citizens found renewed faith in the power of their collective voice, realizing that they held the key to dismantling the oppressive cycle of bribery and neglect.

With every passing day, the campaign's message reverberated through the constituency. Town halls overflowed with impassioned speeches, where citizens shared their stories of hardship and yearning for change. They saw in Benjamin a leader who understood their struggles, a leader who had risen from the same slums and had turned his adversity into an opportunity for transformation.

Benjamin and Lynne stood together on a stage, addressing a crowd of thousands. The air crackled with anticipation as Benjamin's voice boomed through the loudspeakers, declaring his commitment to uprooting corruption and ushering in an era of transparent governance.

The crowd erupted in thunderous applause, their united voices echoing the resounding demand for change. Benjamin's determination, fueled by the truth revealed by Lynne, had struck a chord with the citizens. The battle had only just begun, but they were ready to fight alongside him, armed with the truth, unwavering in their resolve.

As the sun set on that day, the stage was set for the final act—a clash of ideals, a battle for the soul of their constituency. The subsequent realities would bear witness to the fierce struggle that lay ahead, as Benjamin and Lynne confronted powerful adversaries, faced personal sacrifices, and navigated treacherous political landscapes. Their journey would test their resilience, their character, and their unwavering belief in the transformative power of truth and justice.

Chapter 12:

Unity in the Face of Adversity

The atmosphere crackled with tension as Benjamin and his team gathered in a small, dimly lit room, their faces etched with determination. The recent escalation of threats and attempts to derail their campaign had cast a shadow of doubt and fear among them. But instead of succumbing to despair, they chose to rally together, united by a common purpose: to bring about meaningful change.

Benjamin stood at the front of the room; his voice steady but filled with conviction. "We knew this wouldn't be an easy battle," he began, addressing the dedicated group before him. "But we cannot let fear and intimidation stop us from fighting for what is right. Our unity is our greatest strength."

His words resonated with the assembled team, their eyes shining with a renewed sense of purpose. They had come from different walks of life, each with their own struggles and hardships. But in that moment, they saw beyond their differences and recognized the importance of standing together against the corrupt forces that sought to maintain the status quo.

As the days wore on, the threats intensified. Flyers defaming Benjamin appeared on every street corner, rumors and false accusations were spread through word of mouth, and even acts of vandalism were committed against their campaign headquarters. But the resilience of Benjamin's team only grew stronger.

Supporters from all corners of the community rallied around Benjamin, offering their time, resources, and unwavering support. Volunteers spent countless hours distributing campaign materials, canvassing neighborhoods, and engaging in conversations with skeptical voters. The power of unity was on full display as people set aside their differences and came together for a shared cause.

In the face of adversity, Benjamin and Lynne Carrow together with their team found solace in one another's unwavering dedication. They drew strength from the collective belief that change was possible, that their community deserved better. The attempts to divide them only served to strengthen their resolve, as they understood that their fight was not just for themselves, but for the voiceless, the marginalized, and the forgotten.

Through their unity, they found inspiration in the stories of individuals who had been directly impacted by the corrupt practices of those in power. They listened to the struggles of families burdened by poverty, students deprived of educational opportunities, and victims of injustice denied their right to fair treatment. These stories fueled their determination, reminding them of the urgency and importance of their mission.

As the campaign gained momentum, Benjamin's team became a force to be reckoned with. They organized rallies, town hall meetings, and community events, spreading their message of hope, transparency, and accountability. The people began to see the stark contrast between Benjamin and the incumbent Mr. Masur, recognizing the genuine passion and integrity that radiated from Benjamin's every word.

And as the community witnessed their unity, their shared vision, and their unwavering dedication, they too began to rally behind Benjamin. The campaign was no longer just about one person seeking a seat of power; it had become a movement for change, a collective endeavor to reclaim their voice and reshape their future.

In the face of adversity, their unity became a beacon of hope, illuminating a path forward. Together, they stood firm, ready to face whatever challenges lay ahead, knowing that they were not alone. United in their cause, they were determined to rewrite the narrative, to topple the walls of corruption, and to build a community that thrived on justice, compassion, and equality.

Reality marks a turning point in their journey. It was a testament to the power of unity, reminding Benjamin and his team that when they stood together, they were an unstoppable force, capable of overcoming any obstacle in their path.

As the unity among Benjamin's team grew stronger, so did their resilience in the face of adversity. They refused to be intimidated or swayed by the desperate attempts of their opponents. Instead, they channeled their energy into strategic planning, honing their message, and reaching out to the community with unwavering determination.

One evening, as the sun set and cast a warm glow over the bustling campaign office, Benjamin addressed his team. "We have faced countless challenges and obstacles along this journey, but we have come so far," he declared, his voice filled with gratitude and pride. "Each one of you has played a crucial role in building this movement for change, and I am honored to stand beside you."

The room erupted with applause, a testament to the bonds forged through shared hardships and a common goal. Volunteers, young and old, from different backgrounds and walks of life, stood shoulder to shoulder, united by their belief in a better future.

Amidst the clamor of excitement, Benjamin's campaign manager, Lynne Carrow, stepped forward. "We have witnessed the power of unity in action," she said, her voice steady and resolute. "But we must remain vigilant. Our opponents will stop at nothing to undermine our progress and sow discord among us."

Nods of agreement swept through the room as team members exchanged determined glances. They understood the gravity of the moment and the challenges that still lay ahead. They knew that their unity would be tested, but they were committed to facing every trial together.

With renewed focus, the team devised strategies to counteract the smear campaigns, misinformation, and underhanded tactics employed by their adversaries. They launched a comprehensive social media campaign, using the power of digital platforms to disseminate the truth, connect with voters, and debunk falsehoods.

In addition, they organized community events that celebrated diversity and inclusivity, highlighting the shared aspirations and values that united their constituency. These events served as a powerful reminder that, despite their differences, the people were stronger when they stood together.

The unity within Benjamin's team also extended beyond the campaign office. They actively collaborated with other like-minded individuals and grassroots organizations, forming alliances that amplified their collective voice. They reached out to community and clergy leaders, engaged in meaningful conversations with local businesses, and fostered relationships built on trust and mutual respect.

As the campaign gained momentum, the community began to take notice. People who had previously felt disillusioned or apathetic found hope and inspiration in Benjamin's message of integrity and genuine concern for their well-being. They saw in him a leader who would not be swayed by personal gain, but who would remain steadfast in his commitment to serving the people.

The support swelled, stretching beyond political affiliations and transcending socioeconomic divisions. Benjamin's team was no longer just a campaign—it had become a movement. A movement that stood for accountability, transparency, and a government that prioritized the needs of the people.

Reality continued to mark a pivotal moment in their journey—a testament to the power of unity and the unwavering determination to bring about change. They had faced adversity head-on and emerged stronger, ready to confront the remaining challenges with renewed vigor.

As they looked ahead, they knew that the battle was far from over. But with their unity as their shield and their shared vision as their guiding light, they were prepared to forge ahead, steadfast in their pursuit of a brighter future for all. As election day dawned, Benjamin's resolve reached its pinnacle. The culmination of months of hard work, sacrifice, and unwavering determination hung in the balance. The fate of his community, the realization of their aspirations, rested in the hands of the electorate.

Chapter 13:

The Election Day

Election Day dawned with a palpable sense of anticipation and nervous excitement. The community had been swept up in the whirlwind of Benjamin's campaign, drawn to his promise of change and inspired by his unwavering dedication. The stakes were high, not only for Benjamin but for the entire constituency.

As the day unfolded, the streets buzzed with activity. Supporters from both camps adorned themselves with campaign paraphernalia, proudly displaying their allegiance to their chosen candidate. Conversations echoed through every corner, as friends and neighbors engaged in spirited debates, passionately defending their beliefs.

At the heart of it all, the polling stations stood as symbols of democracy in action. Lines snaked around the buildings, with people eagerly waiting their turn to cast their votes, their voices echoing the desire for a brighter future.

In the campaign headquarters, Benjamin and his team gathered, their expressions a mix of hope, anxiety, and determination. They knew that they had given their all, poured their hearts and souls into this fight for justice and equality. But the outcome still hung in the balance, and the uncertainty was both exhilarating and nerve-wracking.

Meanwhile, in a lavish mansion, Mr. Masur nervously paced the floors, his face etched with worry. The corruption that had sustained him for so long now threatened to crumble under the weight of public scrutiny. He was acutely aware that his political dynasty hung in the balance, that the choices he had made would determine not only his fate but that of his family.

As the day wore on, the sun began its descent, casting a golden hue over the landscape. The air was thick with anticipation, each passing moment ratcheting up the tension. Social media platforms buzzed with speculations, exit polls were shared, and the community held its breath, collectively yearning for change.

Nightfall brought a hush over the constituency, a silence that was punctuated only by the sound of ballot boxes being transported to the tallying centers. The fate of the community now lay in the hands of diligent election officials, entrusted with the responsibility of safeguarding the democratic process.

Hours turned into an eternity as the counting process unfolded. Benjamin's supporters anxiously clung to hope, while Mr. Masur's loyalists hoped for a different outcome. The tension was palpable, a reflection of the deep divide within the constituency.

Then, finally, the moment arrived. The election officials stepped forward, their expressions a mix of gravity and solemnity. The room fell into a hushed silence as they prepared to announce the results.

A collective breath was held as the official began to read out the numbers, the crowd straining to catch every word. The margin was close, every vote mattered. The air crackled with anticipation, as if the very future of the community hung in the balance.

And then, the words spilled forth, filling the room with their significance. Benjamin had emerged victorious, his unwavering commitment to change resonating with the hearts and minds of the constituency. The room erupted into cheers and applause, an outpouring of joy and relief.

In that moment, the community stood united, rejoicing in the triumph of hope over apathy, integrity over corruption. Benjamin had not only won an election; he had ignited a spark of transformation that would reverberate through the generations to come.

As the news spread, the streets came alive with celebration. People poured out of their homes, hugging, dancing, and waving flags of victory. It was a moment of collective triumph, a testament to the power of the people and their refusal to be silenced.

For Benjamin, the victory was bittersweet. It marked the beginning of a new chapter, one filled with immense responsibility and challenges. But he stood tall, his heart filled with gratitude for the unwavering support of the community that had placed their trust in him. Benjamin took the stage, his voice ringing with gratitude and determination.

"My brothers and sisters, today is not just a victory for me, but a victory for each and every one of you who believed in the power of change," Benjamin declared, his words echoing through the jubilant crowd. "We have shown that when we stand united, we can overcome any obstacle and create a future that is fair and just for all. I am humbled by your unwavering support," He continued, his voice filled with genuine gratitude. "This victory is not mine alone; it belongs to each and every one of you who stood by my side, who believed in the vision of a community that thrives on justice, equality, and compassion."

The cheering intensified, as Benjamin's supporters reveled in the realization that their voices had been heard, that their votes had made a difference. In that moment, the spirit of unity and hope permeated the air, transcending the boundaries that had once divided the community.

As the night wore on, Benjamin and his team retreated to a quiet corner of the campaign headquarters, where they could reflect on the journey they had undertaken. Emotions ran high, as they recounted the challenges they had faced, the bonds they had forged, and the shared belief in a better tomorrow.

The room fell into a contemplative silence, the weight of their newfound responsibility settling upon their shoulders. They knew that the real work had just begun. There were promises to fulfill, reforms to enact, and the task of rebuilding trust in the political system.

But amidst the challenges, Benjamin and his team found solace in their shared purpose and the unbreakable bond they had formed. They knew that as long as they remained united, guided by integrity and a genuine desire to serve, they could overcome any obstacles that lay in their path.

As dawn broke over the constituency, casting a soft glow on the landscape, Benjamin stepped out onto the balcony of his campaign headquarters. The cheering crowd had long dispersed, but the echoes of their support lingered in the air. The journey had been arduous, but it was a testament to the power of unity, resilience, and the unwavering belief in a brighter future.

On the great election day, the power of corruption clashed with the unwavering spirit of the people. The votes were cast, and the results emerged as a resounding verdict—a verdict that shook the foundation of Mr. Masur's empire. The citizens had spoken, and their voices could no longer be silenced.

As Benjamin emerged victorious, the realization dawned upon the constituency that the era of corruption and greed was coming to an end. A new dawn of accountability and transparency beckoned, and with it came the hope of a brighter future.

The defeat was a humbling blow for Mr. Masur, a man accustomed to wielding power with impunity. As the election results were announced, his empire crumbled around him, and the once-loyal enforcers who had carried out his bidding melted away, leaving him isolated and vulnerable.

For the first time in years, the citizens of southern constituency felt a glimmer of optimism. They dared to dream of a constituency where their voices mattered, where their concerns would be addressed, and where their hard work and dedication would be met with opportunities for growth and prosperity.

Chapter 14:

Redemption and Love

With the election results favoring Benjamin, he emerged victorious and brought hope to the constituency. Lynne Carrow and Benjamin united in marriage, symbolizing the triumph of love, justice, and the people's power.

The sun shone brightly over the constituency on the day of Benjamin's inauguration. The air was filled with a renewed sense of hope and optimism as the community gathered to witness the swearing-in of their new representative. The echoes of their voices merged into a chorus of anticipation, their eyes fixed on the podium where Benjamin stood, ready to take the oath of office.

As Benjamin raised his right hand and solemnly swore to uphold the values of justice and integrity, Lynne Carrow stood beside him, a radiant smile adorning her face. Their union represented more than just a bond of love; it symbolized the unity of purpose and shared ideals that had propelled their journey.

As Benjamin took his oath of office, the weight of responsibility settled on his shoulders. He understood the enormity of the task ahead—rebuilding trust, dismantling the corrupt networks, and working tirelessly to uplift the lives of those who had long been neglected.

The Mutinda family joined Benjamin and Lynne Carrow too, their hearts filled with pride and hope. Their journey from the depths of tragedy to the pinnacle of triumph had not been in vain. Their pain had transformed into a driving force for change, and they were determined to support Benjamin in his quest to reshape the destiny of their community.

Together, Benjamin and Lynne Carrow formed an unbreakable partnership—a union grounded in love, shared values, and a common vision for a constituency that thrived on justice, integrity, and genuine care for its people. Their bond served as a powerful symbol—a testament to the belief that love and compassion could prevail even in the face of deep-rooted corruption.

The road ahead would not be easy. The shadows of Mr. Masur's legacy loomed large, and the fight against corruption would require unwavering dedication, resilience, and the support of the community. But the citizens had spoken, and they were ready to stand behind their newly elected representative, ready to reclaim their voices and forge a path towards a better future.

As Benjamin looked out at the community he now served, he felt a renewed sense of purpose. The challenges ahead were formidable, but he was determined to honor the trust that had been placed in him. The unity that had propelled him to victory would guide him through the trials and tribulations that awaited.

With a deep breath and a smile of quiet resolve, Benjamin stepped forward, ready to embrace the responsibility that came with his new role. He knew that the road ahead would not be easy, but he was prepared to walk it, hand in hand with the community that had embraced the power of unity and refused to accept anything less than the promise of a better future for all.

The ceremony marked a turning point in the constituency's history. The days of corruption, neglect, and broken promises were now firmly behind them. Benjamin's victory had ushered in a new era, one where the people's voices would be heard and their needs prioritized.

In his inaugural address, Benjamin spoke passionately about the community's potential and his unwavering commitment to its welfare. He outlined his plans to tackle the pressing issues that had long plagued the constituency, promising transparency, accountability, and a government that would work tirelessly for the betterment of all.

The crowd erupted in applause, their cheers reverberating through the air, as Benjamin's words resonated with their shared dreams and aspirations. The bond between the community and its new representative grew stronger with each passing moment, their trust in him deepening.

As the ceremony concluded, the celebration continued in the form of a joyous reception. The community came together, sharing laughter, stories, and dances that reflected the vibrant spirit of their shared victory. The atmosphere was electric, filled with an overwhelming sense of camaraderie and the belief that, together, they could overcome any obstacle.

In the midst of the revelry, Lynne Carrow and Benjamin found a moment of respite. They stood hand in hand, gazing into each other's eyes, the journey they had undertaken etched on their faces. Their love had blossomed amidst the chaos and challenges, and now it stood as a beacon of hope and resilience.

"Lynne, none of this would have been possible without you," Benjamin said, his voice filled with gratitude. "Your unwavering support, your belief in me, and your tireless efforts have been the driving force behind our victory. I am honored to stand by your side, not just as your husband but as a partner in the fight for justice and equality."

Lynne Carrow's eyes glistened with emotion as she squeezed Benjamin's hand. "Benjamin, you have shown me the true meaning of courage and determination. Together, we have the power to make a difference, to uplift the lives of those who have been marginalized and forgotten. Our love is not just a personal bond; it is a catalyst for change."

In that moment, as they stood amidst the celebration and the clamor of voices, their love intertwined with the collective love of the community. It was a love that transcended the boundaries of individual hearts, a love that united them in their pursuit of a brighter future.

As the day drew to a close, the stars twinkled overhead, casting a gentle glow on the constituency that had witnessed a profound transformation. The road ahead was long and challenging, but with love as their compass and the unwavering support of the community, Benjamin and Lynne Carrow were ready to face whatever lay ahead.

Together, they would rewrite the narrative of their constituency, breathing life into the promises of progress and justice. They would carry the torch of redemption and love, illuminating the path for generations to come, reminding the world that when hearts unite, change is not just a possibility but an unstoppable force.

The following days were a flurry of activity as Benjamin and Lynne Carrow dove headfirst into their roles as the constituency's representatives. With a shared vision and an unwavering commitment to their community, they embarked on a whirlwind of meetings, discussions, and planning sessions.

Benjamin wasted no time in expediting his campaign promises. He established an open-door policy, encouraging constituents to voice their concerns and share their ideas. With a genuine desire to understand the challenges they faced, he listened attentively, taking note of each individual's story, their struggles, and their aspirations.

Lynne Carrow, with her sharp intellect and unwavering dedication, became a driving force behind the scenes. She brought her expertise and fresh perspectives, analyzing data, researching best practices, and crafting strategies that would ensure the constituency's progress. Her presence was felt not only in the corridors of power but also in the grassroots initiatives that aimed to uplift the most marginalized members of society.

Together, Benjamin and Lynne Carrow spearheaded a series of transformative projects. They invested in education, creating scholarship programs and improving school facilities to ensure that every child had access to quality education. They championed healthcare reforms, working to establish affordable clinics and improve access to medical services in underserved areas. They also prioritized infrastructure development, connecting the dilapidated slums with better roads and promoting sustainable energy solutions.

The community responded with renewed vigor and participation. Citizens, once disillusioned by years of neglect, felt a renewed sense of pride and hope. They rallied around Benjamin and Lynne Carrow, eager to contribute their skills, resources, and time to the collective endeavor of building a better future.

As Benjamin immersed himself further into the intricacies of governance, he sought the guidance of seasoned activists, intellectuals, and grassroots leaders who shared his vision. He recognized the importance of building a strong support network, of surrounding himself with individuals who could provide guidance and lend their expertise to the cause. Together, they formed a formidable coalition, united in their determination to challenge the status quo and effect lasting change. He spent countless hours engaging with citizens, visiting neighborhoods plagued by poverty and neglect, and actively listening to their concerns. Through these interactions, he gained invaluable insights into the lived experiences of his constituents. The depth of their struggles further fueled his resolve, reinforcing his commitment to being their voice in the corridors of power.

With each passing day, Benjamin's resolve solidified. He sought knowledge, immersing himself in the history of his constituency, studying the intricacies of governance and the principles of effective leadership. He recognized the importance of understanding the nuances of policy and the mechanisms that perpetuated inequality, determined to dismantle the very structures that had enabled Mr. Masur's reign.

As Lynne Carrow ventured into the heart of the Southern constituency, Benjamin's wife, confidant and partner encountered individuals whose stories touched her deeply. She listened to the struggles of single mothers grappling with poverty, of children denied access to quality education, and of families torn apart by systemic injustices. Their resilience in the face of adversity ignited a fire within her, propelling her to action. Lynne Carrow worked with Benjamin not only as his wife, but as an individual who wanted to bring a total change to the community.

Driven by a newfound empathy, Lynne Carrow vowed to use her privilege (MP's wife) as a platform for change. She harnessed her eloquence and intellect, passionately articulating the injustices she had witnessed firsthand. Her speeches echoed through crowded halls, resonating with the hearts of those yearning for an activist who would fight for their rights, who would champion their cause.

In her pursuit of justice, Lynne Carrow faced opposition from within her own family. Her father, Mr. Masur, regarded her burgeoning activism as an act of betrayal, a threat to the carefully constructed façade of their fallen power. He sought to quell her dissent, employing tactics of manipulation and intimidation to force her compliance.

But Lynne Carrow would not be silenced. Bolstered by her husband support base, she withstood the storm of her fallen father's disapproval, fueled by an unyielding determination to fight for the truth, regardless of the consequences.

The constituency witnessed tangible changes, small victories that gradually accumulated into a wave of progress. The slums began to transform, as government initiatives and community-driven projects improved living conditions and provided opportunities for economic empowerment. The voices of the marginalized were amplified, their concerns heard and addressed. The cycle of corruption was broken, replaced by a system of transparency and accountability.

In the midst of their demanding schedules and the weight of their responsibilities, Benjamin and Lynne Carrow found solace in each other's presence. Their love not only anchored them but also fueled their determination to leave a lasting legacy. They celebrated each milestone together, drawing strength from their partnership and the shared belief that love, when coupled with action, could shape the course of history.

As the first phase (100 days) of Benjamin's tenure neared its end, the community gathered once again, this time not for a celebration but for a reflection on the progress made. The air was filled with gratitude and a renewed sense of purpose. Benjamin took the stage, his voice resonating with pride as he addressed his constituents.

"My friends, we have come a long way together," he began, his gaze sweeping across the crowd. "We have proven that change is not an abstract concept but a tangible reality that can be achieved when we stand united. Our journey has been filled with challenges, but it is through our collective efforts, our unwavering determination, and our love for this community that we have managed to overcome them."

The crowd erupted into applause, their cheers filling the air, a testament to the transformative power of unity and love. Benjamin continued; his voice unwavering with conviction.

"This is just the beginning. We have laid the foundation for a brighter future, but there is still much work to be done. Let us never forget the power of our collective voice, the strength of our love for one another, and the impact we can have when we work hand in hand. Together, we will continue to build a community that thrives on justice, equality, and compassion."

The applause swelled, echoing far beyond the gathering, reverberating through the hearts and minds of the constituency. Benjamin and Lynne Carrow, standing side by side, looked out at the sea of faces before them. They knew that their journey was far from over, that the road ahead would be filled with obstacles and setbacks. But they also knew that they had something powerful on their side – the unwavering support and determination of a community that had experienced the transformative power of unity.

With renewed vigor and a shared vision, Benjamin and Lynne Carrow embarked on their second phase (200 days) determined to build upon the foundations they had laid. They continued to listen to the needs and aspirations of their constituents, working tirelessly to translate those voices into meaningful action.

Their commitment to transparency and accountability remained unwavering. They established mechanisms to ensure that every taxpayer's money was utilized effectively and efficiently, leaving no room for corruption or misuse. They encouraged active citizen participation in decision-making processes, empowering the community to take ownership of their own development.

But it was not just in the realm of governance that Benjamin and Lynne Carrow made an impact. They understood that true transformation required addressing the root causes of inequality and injustice. They championed initiatives that focused on empowering women, uplifting marginalized groups, and creating opportunities for the youth.

Their efforts bore fruit as the constituency witnessed a wave of socio-economic growth. New businesses thrived, job opportunities expanded, and the gap between the privileged and the marginalized began to narrow. The once-neglected slums transformed into vibrant communities, brimming with hope and opportunity.

Throughout their journey, Benjamin and Lynne Carrow remained steadfast in their love for each other. Their marriage served as a beacon of hope, a reminder that love could not only endure the trials of leadership but also flourish and inspire. Together, they exemplified the power of unity, empathy, and shared values.

As they reflected on their achievements, they knew that their story was not unique. It was a story that resonated with countless communities around the world, where ordinary people rose above adversity and fought for a better future. Their journey was a testament to the enduring spirit of resilience and the unwavering belief in the power of love and justice.

And so, the legacy of Benjamin and Lynne Carrow lived on, etched in the hearts and minds of the community they served. Their story became a source of inspiration, a reminder that change was possible, and that no matter how insurmountable the challenges may seem, love and unity could overcome even the darkest of times.

As the pages of their journey turned, the constituency looked forward to a future filled with hope and promise. And they knew that as long as the spirit of love and unity burned bright, their community would continue to thrive, guided by the indomitable spirit of Benjamin, Lynne Carrow, and all those who believed in the transformative power of love, justice, and the collective pursuit of a better world.

Chapter 15:

Serving the People

In the first 20 days of their second phase in office, Benjamin and Lynne Carrow wasted no time in rolling up their sleeves and getting to work. Their shared vision for a better community fueled their determination to bring about meaningful change and address the pressing needs of their constituents.

They began by conducting a comprehensive assessment of the most critical issues facing the constituency. Through town hall meetings, community surveys, and consultations with experts, they gathered invaluable insights and firsthand accounts of the challenges that needed to be addressed urgently.

With a clear understanding of the community's priorities, Benjamin and Lynne Carrow devised a strategic plan that encompassed a wide range of sectors, from education and healthcare to infrastructure and economic development.

Their first focus was on education. Recognizing that a strong foundation in education was vital for the future of the community, they directed their efforts toward improving school facilities, increasing access to quality education, and supporting teachers through training programs and incentives.

They allocated funds to repair dilapidated schools, ensuring that children had safe and conducive learning environments. They implemented scholarship programs to support academically gifted students from low-income families, giving them the opportunity to pursue higher education and break the cycle of poverty.

In the healthcare sector, Benjamin and Lynne Carrow were determined to address the lack of accessible and affordable medical services. They initiated partnerships with healthcare organizations, both local and international, to establish mobile clinics that would reach remote areas and provide basic healthcare services.

They also worked on improving existing healthcare facilities, equipping them with modern medical equipment and recruiting skilled healthcare professionals. Their aim was to ensure that every citizen had access to quality healthcare without being burdened by exorbitant medical bills.

Infrastructure development was another area of focus for Benjamin and Lynne Carrow. They understood that well-maintained roads, reliable water supply, and efficient waste management systems were crucial for the community's growth and well-being.

They secured funding for road construction and maintenance, aiming to connect all parts of the constituency and improve transportation networks. They collaborated with water management authorities to enhance access to clean and safe water, especially in slums that had been neglected for years.

To address the waste management challenges, Benjamin and Lynne Carrow launched a community-wide campaign to promote waste reduction, recycling, and proper waste disposal practices. They organized clean-up drives and engaged with local businesses and organizations to develop sustainable waste management solutions.

In their relentless pursuit of economic development, Benjamin and Lynne Carrow actively supported local entrepreneurs and small businesses. They established business incubation centers, providing aspiring entrepreneurs with resources, mentorship, and access to capital.

They also sought to attract investments and promote tourism in the region, recognizing the potential for job creation and economic growth. Through strategic partnerships with private enterprises and government agencies, they embarked on initiatives to showcase the constituency's natural beauty, cultural heritage, and economic potential.

Every decision Benjamin and Lynne Carrow made was driven by their commitment to justice, equality, and inclusivity. They championed initiatives that promoted gender equality, youth empowerment, and the rights of marginalized communities. They ensured that women and minority groups had a seat at the table and were actively involved in decision-making processes.

Their second phase in office was marked by tireless efforts, countless meetings, and late nights spent poring over plans and proposals. Benjamin and Lynne Carrow were fueled by their unwavering belief in the power of transformative leadership and the positive impact it could have on the lives of their constituents.

The community, witnessing their dedication and tangible progress, rallied behind Benjamin and Lynne Carrow. Volunteers emerged, offering their time and skills to support the initiatives. Local organizations, businesses, and individuals joined hands with the elected representatives, forging a united front in the pursuit of common goals.

Benjamin and Lynne Carrow established an open-door policy, inviting citizens to share their ideas, concerns, and aspirations. They held regular community meetings, where they listened attentively to the voices of the people they served. Through these interactions, they gained deeper insights into the specific needs of different neighborhoods and demographics within the constituency.

To ensure transparency and accountability, Benjamin and Lynne Carrow implemented a robust system for tracking the utilization of funds allocated to various projects. They made it a priority to regularly update the community on the progress and impact of their initiatives. Monthly reports were shared, detailing the funds spent, milestones achieved, and the challenges encountered along the way.

One of the key projects they initiated in Benjamin's second phase was a youth empowerment program. Recognizing the potential of the younger generation to drive change, they launched skill development workshops, vocational training programs, and entrepreneurship initiatives aimed at nurturing talent and creating employment opportunities.

In their commitment to environmental conservation, they led tree-planting campaigns that aimed to reduce the impact of climate change. They partnered with environmental organizations to address issues such as deforestation, soil erosion, and water pollution.

Furthermore, Benjamin and Lynne Carrow worked tirelessly to improve access to justice for all citizens. They set up legal aid clinics and facilitated community dialogues to promote peaceful resolution of disputes. They also advocated for the strengthening of the judicial system and the protection of human rights, ensuring that every citizen had equal access to justice and fair treatment under the law.

Their dedication to serving the community went beyond their official roles. Benjamin and Lynne Carrow actively participated in community service initiatives, such as volunteering at local schools, organizing health and hygiene campaigns, and supporting charitable organizations. They believed that true leadership meant leading by example and being present in the lives of the people they represented.

As his second phase came to a close, Benjamin and Lynne Carrow reflected on the progress they had made. The seeds of change had been planted, and the community was beginning to witness the tangible results of their collective efforts. The spirit of hope and optimism permeated the air, as citizens saw their aspirations taking shape and their voices being heard.

But Benjamin and Lynne Carrow knew that their work had just begun. They were acutely aware of the challenges that lay ahead and the long road still to be traveled. However, their unwavering determination, coupled with the support and trust of the community, fueled their resolve to continue fighting for a better future.

They remained committed to their vision of a constituency where every individual had equal opportunities, where prosperity was shared, and where the voices of the marginalized were amplified. With renewed energy and a deep sense of purpose, Benjamin and Lynne Carrow looked forward to the days, months, and years ahead, ready to face the challenges, celebrate the victories, and leave a lasting legacy of positive change for generations to come.

Chapter 16:

A Community Transformed

Reality continued to unfold the story of Benjamin's rise as an entrepreneur and political force, showcasing the transformative impact he had on the community. As time moved, the slums witnessed a remarkable shift—a community that had once been defined by despair and poverty now thrived with newfound hope and opportunities.

Benjamin's entrepreneurial endeavors continued to flourish, as did his commitment to social impact. He expanded his business ventures, venturing into new industries and exploring innovative ways to address the pressing needs of the community. From creating employment opportunities to supporting local artisans and fostering sustainable practices, Benjamin's businesses became a catalyst for positive change, uplifting not only the economy but also the social fabric of the constituency.

As Benjamin's political career gained momentum, he tirelessly championed the rights and well-being of the marginalized. He fought for policies that prioritized social welfare, healthcare access, and affordable housing for all. His experiences as an entrepreneur provided him with firsthand insights into the challenges faced by the business community, and he advocated for an enabling environment that supported local entrepreneurs and attracted sustainable investments.

Beyond his policy initiatives, Benjamin remained deeply connected to the community he served. Accompanied by Lynne Carrow, he regularly visited the slums, engaging with residents, listening to their concerns, and taking proactive steps to address their needs. He believed in the power of grassroots movements, empowering the citizens to actively participate in decision-making processes and shaping the policies that directly impacted their lives.

Reality delves into the stories of individuals whose lives were transformed under Benjamin's leadership. Families once trapped in the vicious cycle of poverty now had access to healthcare, education, and economic opportunities. Small businesses flourished, and a spirit of entrepreneurship permeated the slums as more residents were inspired to pursue their dreams.

The community itself underwent a profound transformation. The slums, once neglected and forgotten, became a vibrant hub of innovation, creativity, and resilience. Benjamin's influence extended beyond his own initiatives, as he facilitated partnerships between local businesses, NGOs, and government agencies, fostering collaborations that had a far-reaching impact on the community's development.

Benjamin faced fierce opposition from entrenched interests who resisted change and sought to protect their own vested interests. The forces of corruption and greed continued to lurk in the shadows, threatening to undermine the progress that had been made. Yet, Benjamin remained undeterred, drawing strength from the unwavering support of the community and his unyielding belief in the power of collective action.

A sense of optimism pervaded the realities. The slums had become a symbol of resilience, hope, and transformation—a testament to what could be achieved when a community united under a visionary leader. Benjamin's journey as an entrepreneur and political force had become inseparable from the journey of the community itself, as they walked hand in hand toward a brighter future.

Going forward, reality would unveil the climax of Benjamin's story, the ultimate test of his leadership and the realization of his vision. With each move, reality would witness the culmination of his efforts, the triumphs, and the sacrifices made along the way. And as the narrative unfolded, the true power of an individual committed to bringing about change would shine through—a power that could transform not only a community but the very fabric of society itself.

Chapter 17:

True Justice

"As the father of Lynne Carrow, I have grappled with the knowledge of my own shortcomings and the impact they have had on my family and community. I stand humbled by the strength and conviction of my daughter, who, driven by a sense of justice, dared to challenge the very foundation upon which our family's prosperity was built." Mr. Masur said these words in a court of law when he was convicted of misusing public funds while he was in power.

The court room was full of people from different fields and fraternities who had come to hear the case which had been filed by one of the citizens from the constituency he once represented as a member of parliament. His own daughter and blood: Lynne Carrow Benjamin. Mr. Masur pleaded guilty on all the charges which had been placed upon him.

The Central Law court Judge, with his voice raised up, convinced with her verdict, "The verdict of this hearing, now becomes the judgement of this honorable court. But before everything, I want you to know that the beauty of a legal system is overall that it works for the good of every citizen. If we realize that it's not working at some point, we don't have a right to take a corrective measure. Especially in corruption cases, if we do so, we will not have a justice society. Mr. Masur, I pronounce you guilt for the crime you have been convicted with; misusing public funds while in office. Your actions were not only criminal, but also a total betrayal to the people who entrusted you with the heart of their constituency. As a warning to others who possess similar behavior like yours, this court has sentenced you for 15 years in jail."

About the author

Jouvenalliss Mwendwa Kioko is a remarkable individual who embodies the qualities of a man of God, life coach, mentor, and writer. Renowned for his training expertise and extensive global travels, he has dedicated his life to researching and imparting wisdom on various aspects of life. With a broad range of experience spanning fields such as insurance, sales and marketing, hospitality, telecommunications, manufacturing, and oil and gas, Jouvenalliss has made an impact both locally and internationally. As an accomplished author, he has penned several insightful books, including **"The Scar of Destiny," "English speaking & writing," "Resources & Mechanics of Marriage," "Fall to Fly," "Boulevard of Success," "Oomph Bells," "Spry Detective," "The Mock Pal," and "Jezebel,"** with many more upcoming works in the pipeline. His written works delve into diverse subjects, touching on personal growth, relationships, success, and overcoming adversity.

Jouvenalliss' journey to success is a testament to his unwavering determination and faith in God. Born in the slums of Kibra, Nairobi, Kenya, he grew up in various estates in Nairobi, including Dandora, Mathare, Zimmerman, Githurai, Embakasi, and Pipeline. Despite facing significant challenges, he refused to let adversity define him and never gave up on his goals and dreams. Through prayer and unwavering faith, he found the strength to persevere. At the heart of Jouvenalliss' endeavors lies his vision of helping others grow. He has become an emblem of eminence and persistence through his unique approach to tackling challenges. Whenever he faced moments of doubt or the temptation to quit, he would draw upon his grand vision and rise above the immediate obstacles. His unwavering focus and determination have propelled him forward, inspiring those around him to pursue their own aspirations.

As the founder, Crew Party Chief, and CEO of Apton Crew International Ltd (ACIL), Jouvenalliss continues to make a significant impact. Additionally, he holds a graduate certificate in TESOL from the university of Birmingham, United Kingdom and is a graduate of the Holstein Training and Technologies Institute as a Safety Analyst. In his personal life, Jouvenalliss is happily married to Zemenay Mwendwa, and together they are proud parents to their children, Brummelhuis and Beelbright. His commitment to his family and his passion for uplifting others exemplify his character and values.

Jouvenalliss Mwendwa Kioko stands as a beacon of hope, resilience, and unwavering determination. Through his multifaceted roles as a man of God, life coach, mentor, and writer, he continues to inspire individuals from all walks of life to overcome adversity and achieve greatness.